I've known Caz for more than thirty years. He is a man of vision and passion. When others were standing on the sidelines complaining, Caz was in the arena, making it happen. His vision for using recreation to change lives was revolutionary. UPWARD is the premiere sports and recreation ministry in the land. It started in the heart of one man who decided it was time to ACT.

With the release of, *Act or React*, Caz is giving us insights into what drives him as a leader. His insights are clear and concise. It's based on years of observations on how life works. These leadership principles are a must read for those who want to stop the knee jerk reactions and get ahead in the game. The wisdom here will work in any arena. These insights are gleaned in the context of a man who loves God, serves God and is being used by God.

—Dr. Michael Catt, Senior Pastor,
Sherwood Baptist Church

As he has done throughout his ministry, Caz McCaslin uses a combination of facts and personal stories as well as the life and teachings of Christ to inspire us to use our gifts and talents to focus on others. His book challenges us to move beyond our "it's all about me" thinking and transition to a life of serving others, ready to do whatever God asks. I'm recommending this book to all those who want to move from good intentions to doing what God has gifted and prepared them to do. I am grateful for Caz's ministry, his friendship and for his influence in the kingdom.

—Bryant Wright, Senior Pastor,
Johnson's Ferry Baptist Church

Too many people just react to life. They hear the news, take the hits, and stumble into blessings with no real plan or purpose. That's easy. The hard part is reacting well, taking what life gives you and turning it into something meaningful, something to impact the kingdom. If you're ready to turn your reactions into action, this is the book for you.

—Dave Ramsey, *New York Times* best-selling author and nationally syndicated radio show host

One of the main words that captures my heart in Caz's book is "intentional." If we ever hope to redeem our God given opportunities and learn to passionately act when these doors are open, we must "act" now. This book is all about "IMPACT." Read it and implement in your life.

—Dr. Johnny Hunt, Senior Pastor, Woodstock Baptist Church

ACT OR REACT?

ACT OR REACT?

THE DECISION IS OURS

CAZ McCASLIN
Founder of UPWARD SPORTS

NASHVILLE, TENNESSEE

978-1-4336-0694-6

Published by B&H Publishing Group
Nashville, Tennessee

1 2 3 4 5 6 7 • 18 17 16 15 14

I would like to dedicate this book to my precious mother who met Jesus face-to-face on September 6, 2013 and was INTENTIONAL about sharing Jesus with everyone she met until that very moment.

Acknowledgments

How in the world could I ever thank all of the people who helped make this book a reality?

I am so thankful for my Savior who lives through me, my wife Leslie beside me, my children behind me, the Upward Sports Board who is over me, my team who is under me, and the opportunities that are before me. Throughout the development of this book, these folks have provided wisdom and illustrations that have caused me to grow closer to my heavenly Father and have challenged me to be more intentional in every area of my life.

I am also so very thankful for the many long hours and giftedness of Cristie Wisecarver. Without her patience with my schedule and her diligence in compiling the content from all of my notes, it truly just would not have come together. Thank you so much for taking all of this information and clearly putting it into written form. You are simply the best.

Thank you to all of you from the bottom of my heart.

Contents

PHASE TWO: ACT

—It's not about me anymore—
... *and I no longer live, but Christ lives in me. (Galatians 2:20)*

Introduction

"If you want something you've never had, you must be willing to do something you've never done."

When American Founding Father, Thomas Jefferson, uttered those words he knew the weight they carried; he knew what real change required.

According to the USCB (United States Census Bureau), there are seven billion people in the world today. There are more people on the planet than ever before and yet the church is in decline. There's something concerning about that. Today, the market is bigger and yet the church is smaller. Why?

I believe there are several factors which contribute to the church's weakening state, but the one which troubles me the most is the condition of our relationships. Society as a whole doesn't seem to want to invest in others. Very few want to take the time necessary to cultivate meaningful relationships. Many businesses as well as individuals are preoccupied with how many people they can touch—how many friends they have on Facebook or how many followers they have on Twitter. These things, in and of themselves, are not innately *bad*. But they do make me wonder how the ease of communication has impacted our relationships. Are real connections and real interactions a thing of the past? In our attempts to talk more have we simply begun to connect less?

Relationships take perseverance, dedication, compromise, time, and commitment (and those are just a few of the requirements). Relationships are tough. And truly, there's never a point we say, "Okay, we've arrived. We can stop trying now."

I've been married to my beautiful bride for twenty-eight years. Do we have it all figured out? No way. Do we work at it every single day? Absolutely.

About eight years ago, I brought home a horse. (That's pretty much how the story goes when my wife tells it. To her, I think that sums it all up: "He bought a horse.") So yes, after a trip to Tennessee with a friend of mine, I came home with a horse. Now you've got to know something important about me: I don't care if it's racquetball, soccer, volleyball, shooting skeet, or watching NASCAR—I mean it doesn't matter what it is. If I have a buddy who wants to go do something with me, I will go do it! If someone wants to play tennis, and I don't play, I will go buy a racquet just so I can play tennis with my friend.

So this buddy of mine rides horses. (You see where this is going.) And he called me up one day to ask if I would go to Tennessee with him so he could buy a horse. I said, "What in the world do you need another horse for?" He said, "So my friends can ride with me." That sure sounded familiar to me, so I said, "Sure I'll go! And I'll make a deal with you: If you feed the horse, take care of the horse, and give the horse a place to live, the least I can do is buy the horse. I'll buy the horse for myself. I'd love to be able to ride with you anytime I wanted."

Long story short, my loving wife of twenty-eight years, Leslie, was less than pleased by this. It may have been because she found out from a friend instead of me. You see, someone sent her a text with a picture of my new horse, so it kind of came across as, "Look! Caz just bought a horse!" That wasn't exactly how I was going to tell her. I was going to explain to her I was investing in the fellowship of a friend, not simply buying a horse.

So you get it when I say if a friend wants to hunt, fish, play tennis, or ride horses, I'm there—whatever it takes! Over the years, you can imagine my passion for my spending time with friends has caused strain on my marriage—definitely something we've had to work through over and over again. I tell this story now, eight years later, because we can both sit back and laugh (for the most part). But let me assure you, there was no laughing for a long time. We had to really dig in and work. It took effort to get to the other side. And that's a relationship. That's what you have to do. Dig in and work and never give up. You may have good times, and you may have bad times, but at the end of the day you come together and work it out.

E-mail, Facebook, texts, and Twitter have changed the way we interact with one another. What if I e-mailed Leslie my apologies? Instead of a face-to-face conversation, imagine if I tweeted, "Honey, I'm sorry." What do you think might have happened?

Certainly, texting and e-mailing make life easier, but at what expense? We can e-mail instead of meet; we can text instead of talk; we can have two thousand friends on Facebook instead of fifty real, honest-to-goodness relationships. The ability to nurture a true relationship is slipping through our texting fingers.

Now don't get me wrong, technology is great. What would we do without it? I personally have an iPhone and iPad, and would buy an iWhatever-else-there-is. But I think there's something to be said about how we use technology. An app shouldn't replace the actual function of going to church, but it, in essence, is doing just that.

We've made it so easy, people don't have to go to an actual church anymore. With the onset of XM radio and podcasts, we really don't have to darken the doors of an actual church to get what we need. In thirty minutes or less, with an app and a podcast, we can feel ready and spiritually prepared for the week ahead. All we need is the almighty smartphone, and we're set to go!

Technology has not only made it easy to disconnect from real people, but to also stay home and get what we need, creating a larger chasm between the church and its people.

The state of our relationships today is troubling, but I think it's merely a symptom of the real, underlying problem. I think it indicates how people live, how they think, and what they value. Did you know the Oxford Dictionary's word of the year was *selfie* in 2013? Kind of hits the nail on the head, doesn't it?

We, generally speaking, are self-involved and self-centered. The disintegration of relationships is a product of that, hence the decline of the church.

So what do we do? I think it starts with changing our perspective. Instead of being content to sit back and react, we step up and act.

Over the course of this book I want to take you on a journey through two phases. These two phases, *React* and *Act*, hold within them five stages we undergo which transform us from being self-focused to others-focused, teaching us how to be more available, more connected, and more intentional.

In Phase One, the reactive phase, we move through a period where we learn, connect, and grow. This phase is emotionally driven and centers on how others impact us. This phase is imperative because we become impassioned and gain insight in this stage. Without Phase One, Phase Two lacks heart and direction.

Here are the stages in Phase One:

1. Awareness
2. Passion
3. Vision

Within the confines of these three stages, we react to life around us. We don't have to go anywhere or put anything into action.

Let me give you an example. Let's say I've never heard of caramel apples, but you have. So one day you give me a caramel apple. I am now aware on a personal level about the existence, taste, and smell of caramel apples because my friend gave me one to try. And now I love caramel apples! I can't get enough of them. I now have a passion for caramel apples and I want everyone I know to try one. I start thinking what it would be like if I could give a caramel apple to everyone I know. I begin to wonder how I could share what I have with those around me. With this, I begin to imagine what could happen.

Often, that is where it stops because it's easier to sit back and allow things to happen than it is to apply what we've learned and make it grow. So we cycle back through awareness, passion, and vision, reacting to whatever comes our way.

If we decide to stay in Phase One, it's all about us and how we can be impacted by the actions of those around us. However, if we decide to act on our vision, we move into Phase Two.

Here are the stages in Phase Two:

1. Readiness
2. Intentionality

In Phase Two, we are making a conscious effort to impact others. We don't want to keep all the caramel apples to ourselves, so we decide to get ready and intentionally do whatever God tells us to.

This is the point of impact, and this is the place that produces awareness in others. The cycle begins again with the hope our intentional actions cause awareness in someone else—an awareness that prods them to put their vision into practice and ultimately impact someone else. It's a domino effect.

But if we want things to be different, we are going to have to alter what we are doing. We can't keep doing the same things expecting to see different results. I have this theory: It's not what you have that counts, but rather what you do with what you have that matters. If you're intentional, things will happen. If you're not, they won't. It's as simple as that.

You may recall the book by Rick Warren, *The Purpose Driven Life*. The first line, the best line in the entire book is, "It's not about you." What a line! It's not about me! Maybe that's what we need here: a paradigm shift, a new way of thinking about things. What if (now stay with me here), what if we looked at church differently? What if we asked not what can the church do for me, but rather what can I do for the church? What would happen if we all got really intentional and became Jesus with skin on? Perhaps we are not put on this earth to live life for ourselves. Maybe our calling is bigger.

A few years ago, I was in Georgia at a speaking engagement minding my own business. Meanwhile, back at home, my beautiful bride was busy redoing my home office. I think she watched too many episodes of *While You Were Out*, because when I returned my office was transformed! She hung this and painted that. I was floored! And, my very favorite thing was the quote she painted on the wall:

> Jesus Christ understood the concept:
>
> If you want something you've never had, you must be willing to do something you've never done.

Man, does she know me or what? Every day I can look at that quote and be reminded of what it takes to make a difference. What Thomas Jefferson intended for a new country, Paul first envisioned for the church when he said,

"I have been crucified with Christ and I no longer live, but Christ lives in me" (Gal. 2:20).

This life is not about us anymore. Once we become a Christian, it's not about us and our wants and needs. It's about others; it's about connecting and creating relationships with those we come into contact with.

There are people in this world, in our very own cities and towns, who are hurting, searching, and looking for a real connection. What do we do? Text them, Tweet them, or do we stop long enough to listen and connect? *The decision is ours: Are we content to sit back and react, or is it time to step up and act?*

PHASE ONE: REACT

—It's all about me—

I've been crucified with Christ . . .

Awareness (noun)

The state or condition of being aware; having knowledge; consciousness

Aware (adjective)

Having knowledge or perception of a situation or fact; concerned and well-informed about a particular situation or development

> *There can be no knowledge without emotion. We may be aware of a truth, yet until we have felt its force, it is not ours.*
> —Arnold Bennett

CHAPTER ONE

Rayford

Awareness is a great motivator for change. Often, we don't know we need to be aware of something until it's staring us right in the face. And even then, if we aren't paying attention, we will miss it. This concept first came to me while I was in college.

I transferred to the University of Georgia my junior year to finish my degree (Go Dawgs!). I knew I wanted to become a church rec guy, so I got my associate's at Truett-McConnell Junior College then headed to UGA to get my BA in Education with a major in Recreational Leisure.

When I arrived, I met with my advisor. I wasn't really excited about being the new guy on campus. I knew everyone in that major had been together for the last two years, and now here I come. I knew it wasn't going to be easy. But he put me in a class, a small class (one like I was used to at Truett), and told me these were the people to get to know. These were the people I would be with for the next two years. If I could make friends in that class, I would be all set.

I was psyched up for that first class. I got there twenty minutes early to scope out the place. (Just a side note, no one should ever arrive twenty minutes early to any college class. I know this now.) At any rate, I picked the seat right in the center of the room, knowing someone would have to sit beside me one way or another. Slowly, people started coming in and sitting down—but nowhere near me, not behind me, beside or in front of me. Right before class started, I looked around and saw the only empty chairs in the room were the ones—you guessed it—beside me! No one was sitting there, almost purposefully. I thought, *Great. I've got "new guy" plastered all over my forehead.* Then, it all changed . . .

In walked Rayford Nugent. This guy strutted in like he owned the place. His shirt was pressed, he had new kicks on, and he was even working a little bling in his ear and around his neck. You could tell he had it together. He nodded his head to one guy, smiled at the prettiest girl in the room, and since every seat was taken, Rayford headed my way.

When he sat down beside me, I have to admit I was a little unnerved. I realized quickly this guy was the guy to know. I had a chance to make an impression. But before I could say or do anything, this guy looked over at me, gave me a head-nod, and said, "Sup." And as cool as I could be, I nodded back and said, "Sup."

I don't know why, I don't know how, but with one word (and not even a real word) Rayford and I clicked. One day after class he asked me to play ball. And from that point on, for the next two years, if there was a sport to play on campus, we were there. Golf, football, basketball, it didn't matter—you name it, we played it!

Leslie and I were married my senior year of college. Even after getting married, Rayford and I would figure out a way to keep playing the sports we loved. It was great.

Many times, Rayford would ask me to go play golf on a Sunday morning. I'd say, "Gotta go to the churchhouse." After a game, he would ask me to go to a party. I would say something like, "Nah, gonna go hit the books." But Rayford never treated me differently for the decisions I made, and I never treated him differently for the decisions he made. As a matter of fact, we really never talked about it. He did his thing and I did mine. We had a mutual respect for each other. And that was that.

Two years passed. We were in the last week of school, right in the middle of finals. I received a call from a church I'd been interviewing with in South Carolina. They said, "Caz, we'd like to offer you the job as Minister of Recreation." My wife and I were so excited! We were ready-to-go. And by ready-to-go, I mean we ran out that night, rented a U-Haul truck, and loaded it with everything we owned.

After about thirty minutes, everything we owned was in the U-Haul (needless to say, renting a truck was overkill). Nevertheless, I looked at my wife and said, "Honey, I can't believe we get to move to Spartanburg, work at a church, and teach people how to use sports as a tool to share the love of Jesus Christ!"

No sooner had the words left my lips, I realized I couldn't go into a church and teach people how to use sports to reach others when I neglected to do exactly that with my best friend. It was right then and there I became aware of what had been in front of me the entire time: It was my responsibility to share Christ with Rayford. He was my best friend, and yet I'd failed to mention the love of Jesus to him.

My wife and I decided I had to find Rayford before we left. So I did. And buddy, I rolled out every Scripture, every testimony, every story I could think of. I talked for an hour and a half! And I ended with something like this: "Jesus Christ is the most important thing in my life. He should be the most important thing in yours too."

I felt good about how I presented the gospel to Rayford. I was giving myself a mental pat-on-the-back for my good deed, for the way I so eloquently told him about the love of Jesus.

Well, he stopped me dead in my tracks when he spoke. I mean he wasn't judgmental or harsh; he was really just curious. He looked at me with a question on his face and said, "Man, I know everything about you. I know about your mom, your sisters, I even know about your dog. So if this is the most important thing to you, why did it take you two years to tell me about it?"

Words can't express what I felt in that moment: stunned, floored, disappointed. All I could say was, "Rayford, that's my fault. I know I should have said something much sooner."

And not hatefully, not spitefully, and after hours of talking, Rayford said, "I don't need your Jesus."

The next day, I got in my U-Haul and had Rayford in my rearview mirror the whole way to South Carolina. I was heartbroken because I knew my friend did not know Jesus.

What if I had been more aware of my responsibility to share Christ with him? What if I had taken it upon myself to tell him about the love of Jesus? Not until I was called to be a minister at a church did I become aware of the fact it was *my* responsibility as a Christian to share the love of Jesus with those in my circle of influence.

I don't know why I wasn't more aware of that responsibility earlier. Maybe I was too involved with *me* to notice *him*. I guess the focus was on what I could *get* out of the relationship instead of on what I could *give*.

Looking back, it's clear both eyes were not fixed on what was plainly in front of me—my friend.

Often, we don't know we need to be aware of something until it's staring us right in the face. And even then, if we aren't paying attention, we will miss it.

And I missed it then.

But it makes me aware now.

CHAPTER TWO

2,000 Friends?

Why is it so important to us, almost like a badge of honor, to have a lot of friends on Facebook? I don't even have a Facebook account, but I do have three daughters. (Need I say more?) I've seen how it works. I've heard the conversations. It's crazy—865 friends, really?

Have you ever wondered about this Facebook phenomenon? Has its impact on society ever crossed your mind? Well, it has mine. So I looked into it, and do you know what I found? A lot of people use Facebook! (Probably didn't need me to tell you that one, huh?) But seriously, look at these stats. In October of 2012, Facebook disclosed its earnings in its quarterly earnings report and gave its own *status update*:

- 1 million users—End of 2004
- 5.5 million users—End of 2005
- 12 million users—End of 2006
- 20 million users—April 2007

- 200 million users—April 2009
- 1.01 billion users—September 2012

Beyond those staggering numbers, Facebook claims it had an average of 584 million active users each day in the month of September 2012, and 604 million using Facebook from a mobile device each month. Wow! Clearly, the guys at Facebook are on to something.

Now I get why so many people flock to an easy-to-use social outlet; but I wonder about the depth, the real personal connection people have, or think they have, via modes like Facebook.

The desire to feel connected with others is woven into the fabric of human nature. We have a deep-seated need to connect with others. I think Facebook fills this need and gives us a sense of connectedness, real or perceived. I believe that's the reason so many are drawn to Facebook. We want to belong. We want to connect.

I grew up in a military family. My dad was in the army; he served for over thirty years. When he retired, we moved from Washington State to Georgia. I was in the fourth grade, the perfect age to begin watching football with my dad. So when we moved to Georgia, my dad and I would watch a lot of Georgia games. We became huge fans. I grew up watching these guys play; I grew up loving Georgia football.

I remember the first time I walked inside that stadium as an official University of Georgia college student. Ninety-two thousand screaming fans were in the stands. The excitement was overwhelming. Standing there with the kind of fans I'd been watching on TV for years drew me in deeper. If I wasn't a Bulldog fan before, I was after that! I connected with people face-to-face. I felt, maybe for the first time, what it was like to be part of something big.

I believe we are social beings. God created us to have relationships with each other and with Him. I think one of the reasons He has given us these earthly relationships is so we can better understand what it's like to have a relationship with Him. Developing earthly relationships, that is, cultivating them, learning how to listen, and learning how to love, can only enhance our relationship with Jesus Christ. If we lose the ability to communicate with people, and if we lose the skill to connect with others, what can then be said of our relationship with Christ?

Robin Dunbar, a professor at Oxford University, coined the term *Dunbar's Number* in the '90s. Basically, he developed the theory that the human brain can only manage about 150 stable relationships. Now that number varies from 100–230, but even on the high end, 230 is a far cry from what I've seen on Facebook—230 would be mocked! "What's wrong with you? Why don't you have any Facebook friends?" I can just hear the teenage girls now.

Let's go back and take a look at this a minute. This number, 150, represents the people we know and keep in current, social contact with. Those are the parameters of his study. It does not include past social relationships or people we know in a general sense. These 150 would be considered real relationships. I wonder how Facebook (and anyone below the age of forty) would view that finding. I bet they would dispute it. I bet they would think it's completely possible to have tons of friends on Facebook, and otherwise.

Well, in 2011, to disprove *Dunbar's Number* and prove we can have thousands of friends, Rick Lax tried to connect with all two thousand of his Facebook friends. He, alphabetically, went through his Friends List and wrote personal messages to each friend. Beginning with the A's . . .

After getting about halfway through his list, he found most were either surprised or confused to hear from him. He even had one friend he tried to contact who was dead. Can you imagine? (He saw several posts like, "We will miss you," on the News Feed, but just figured the guy was going out of the country or something.) Through the individual messages, he was able to mend a few hurt feelings and send belated birthday wishes to a couple of people. Some responded back to him with a quick life synopsis. Some said, "It's great to hear from you!" But some didn't respond at all. One even said, "I'm sorry. I think you sent this message to me by mistake. I don't think we know each other. LOL!"

Facebook, Twitter, and even texting have made relationships so easy that they've become superficial. No one can have two thousand friends. Not real friends, not real relationships. And listen, I want to be clear here. I'm all for making things easier. I would even say I love technology and what it can do for us. But that kind of communication cannot take the place of connecting face-to-face with people. In order to become "Jesus with skin on," we've got to do more than text; we've got to be willing to do whatever it takes to meet people where they are.

Remember my horse, my tennis racquet, my love of fishing, golf, skeet shooting, soccer, etc.? None of those are important to me if I'm not doing them with a friend. I'm not going to go duck hunting by myself. I'm not going to go play racquetball alone. I don't play sports for the sport in and of itself. I love sports because I get to hang out with my friends. And I think a lot of people are this way. We want to connect.

A man I know through Upward Sports told me this story:

> Back in January, I went to my son's basketball game to watch him play. I'm sitting there in the stands cheering for my boy. The man beside me is cheering for his. I realize quickly our kids are on the same team, so I strike up a conversation with this man I'd never met before.
>
> "Hey, which one is yours?" I ask. "Number 15," he says. "Man, your kid is quite a player. Looks like he's having fun out there," I say. "Yeah, he loves this stuff," he replies. So we cheer for our kids, chat a little about this and that, and after the game we decide to take the boys out for burgers.
>
> The next week, I seek him out. We sit together, and then take the boys out for pizza after the game. So after a few weeks of burgers, pizza, and ice cream, I look over at my friend and say, "Do you guys go to church anywhere around here? He said, "Uh, no. I mean, you know how those church people are." I said, "Those church people aren't so bad. They're kind of like me and you. We go to church right here—same place the boys play basketball. You guys should come this

Sunday." So he agrees to meet me at church the next day.

I find a seat for him and his son, we sit together, sing together; they really seem like they are enjoying themselves. So I look over and ask, "What do you think?" He says, "These church people are pretty cool." I smile, nod my head, and lean back over to say, "Great. Wait right here. I'll be back in a few minutes." My friend says, "Where are you going?" And I say, "I'm going to preach." As I walk to the pulpit I hear him grumbling and laughing at the same time saying, "You're the preacher? The preacher—seriously? The preacher?"

As a pastor, I'd been trying to reach out to the community, trying to find those who did not have a church home. I'd been looking for those who needed to see the love of Jesus. And do you know what I found? Lo and behold, these people I'd been looking for were coming to me. Every Saturday, and once during the week, Upward was bringing me exactly who I'd been looking for.

That man came to church because he was my friend, not because I was the pastor. He came because we developed a relationship. I don't think people are looking for a friendly church; they are looking for a friend.

That's what happened, and that's one of the reasons I love Upward.

If we are going to be Jesus with skin on, we need both eyes wide open to see what's going on around us. Using social outlets like Facebook and Twitter are great, if they are accompanied by real, face-to-face interactions. But in and of themselves, they are not enough. People need more.

We need to be aware of every opportunity that presents itself. Remember my friend, Rayford? We hung out, we played sports. I thought we were tight. But looking back, I guess we weren't, not on a deep level, anyway.

Thirty years ago, Facebook and Twitter weren't around, so why was connecting with him an issue? After all, technology is the problem, right?

Well, not exactly. Facebook, Twitter, e-mail, texts, and anything else that make it easier to communicate are not the problem. Thirty years ago, the problem was me. I chose not to go deeper. I chose to keep our relationship fun and superficial. I had numerous opportunities to share with him but I chose not to. I didn't take advantage of the opportunities presented to me.

But we must strive to. We must make the most out of every opportunity we have to connect with others. We never know which one will click and change someone's life forever.

CHAPTER THREE

It's Not About Me

Despite our differences, we all come into this world the same. With some people we encounter it's easy to think the similarities end there, but they don't. We may take different paths and explore different routes, which shape us in unique ways. Nonetheless, the stages we go through are very much the same for each and every one of us. I've charted out four stages for you:

Stage 1: Everyone Is Like Me
Stage 2: *Not* Everyone Is Like Me
Stage 3: Nobody Is Like Me
Stage 4: Nobody Is Like Me and That's How God
    Planned It

Everyone Is Like Me. When we are little, we develop strong connections with those around us. In particular, children develop strong associations with their mothers. They begin to see similarities, "I have long hair, just like you. I like pink, and you like pink too." In this phase of development, children assume everyone sees life as they do.

Life is concrete and literal. You had better mean exactly what you say when you speak to a child, because what you say is what they're going do. My daughter Keighlee used to have this habit of taking her shoes and socks off when she arrived each day to preschool. The teacher did all she could, but Keighlee just wouldn't listen. Shoes and socks had to be off! Well, her mother and I had to sit her down and have a conversation with her about this. We were very clear on our expectations and were certain she would leave her shoes and socks on the next day.

When we arrived to school the following day, I took the teacher aside to explain what my wife and I had told Keighlee the night before. Well, in the time it took for me to explain our brilliant parenting plan to the teacher, I saw my daughter standing on top of the slide . . . stark naked! With the biggest smile I'd ever seen, she waved and said, "Look, Daddy. I kept my shoes and socks on!" And she did! (And that was all she kept on.)

Life is not only literal, but it's lived in the present during Stage One. Don't ever say to a child, "Your birthday party is only three weeks away," because for the next twenty-one days you will hear, "Is my party today? Is it now? What about today?" They have no frame of reference for the future. Life is lived in the present moment.

Not *Everyone Is Like Me*. During Stage Two, children begin to realize people are different. Everyone might not like pink or have long hair. Everyone might not be black or white or speak the same. I like to think of it like this: Children at this age are judgmental in a nonjudgmental way. What I mean by that is children may see someone in a wheelchair, recognize that as being different from them, and point. They may shout, "Mommy, look! That's different. She has wheels on her chair." Although the mother is mortified, there is not a single bad thought or an ill intent of any kind in the child's mind. All the child sees is a chair with wheels on it. (Then they think, *Man, I wish I had wheels on my chair! That's awesome!*)

At this stage, children begin to understand there are varying ways to look at life. They begin to recognize events occur outside their own lives and life is a little bigger than what they first thought. They realize things relate differently to one another though concepts like, if 3 + 4 = 7, then 7 − 4 = 3. Their worldview is expanding. Kids are wide-eyed and eager to learn more.

Toward the end of this phase, children become a little less egocentric. They begin to appreciate the fact those around them might have needs of their own. This can be such a wonderful time because you start to see maturity emerge. Traits like love, grace, and empathy begin to shine through.

Nobody Is Like Me. I've heard parents say, "It's like one day they are your sweet, loving child, then the next day they turn into someone you don't recognize." Suddenly, they are full of angst, emotion, and uncertainty." Enter the dreaded tweens and teens. This phase is where self-esteem is either built or destroyed. Many kids ask questions like, "Is it okay I look like this? If I wear my hair this way, what are they going to think?" It's an incredibly tough time for kids and for parents. The world has the platform now. It's no longer the parents' opinions, but everyone else's, that matter most.

During this time, our children curiously study those around them and question who they are in relation to those they see. Egocentric thinking takes center stage once again, but now it's colored by what their peers think. In order to figure out who they are, many kids compare themselves to others. Many look to those around them and wonder, "Who am I? I'm certainly not like him or her, so where does that leave me?"

Nobody Is Like Me and That's How God Planned It. Just when you think, as a parent, you can't take anymore, a switch flips, Stage Four hits, and everything seems to settle down. This is when young adults learn to say, "It's okay to be exactly who I am. God has blessed me differently than you, and that's fine with me." This is the place we want our children to be when it's all said and done; this is where we want our children to land.

Unfortunately, some do not. In this world today, there are many fifty- and sixty-year-olds stuck in Stage Three, seeking approval from others and doing all they can to serve the almighty I. There are many who never get the opportunity to see how unique and wonderful they truly are. You see (for those of you who have kids under the age of sixteen), there is no actual switch that flips when kids turn seventeen. Moving from Stage Three to Stage Four requires maturity, reflection, and character development. This can happen at seventeen or seventy.

As I have watched my three daughters grow up, I've seen each of them realize these phases at different times. "Hey, everybody is just like me," is one of my favorites. It didn't matter if the person was red, yellow, young, or old; my girls would run up to just about anyone at any time and hug on them because they thought, "Everyone's just like me."

The older they got, they realized, "Hmm . . . He's a different color than I am. She's older than I am. He rolls around in a wheelchair. My chair doesn't have wheels." After some time they began to question, "Why is nobody like me?" This is a time, unfortunately, when some kids want to back up and be just like everyone else again. It's just too hard to find themselves and be okay with who they are. This may be due in part to a lack of support at home; they may not have someone in their corner cheering them on. It's at this stage a lot of people get stuck, whether it's lack of support, lack of perspective to see the big picture, or lack of understanding how wonderful and unique they are. Many people stay focused right here on self. They try to please others; they try to gain praise and reinforcement from the outside in, as opposed to the inside out. Seeing my daughters move out of "It's all about me," and move into "How can I serve someone else?" is one of the most rewarding evolutions to witness as a father. Watching my daughters become aware of those around them, aware of how they can serve others is, quite honestly, one of the most humbling and joyous experiences of my life.

But I've seen my daughters struggle with this, just as I have struggled with it. It's not easy to keep the focus on others when we live in a society that conditions us to focus on self. Their mere names say it all: iPhone, iPod, iTunes . . . iMean, come on!

I have no qualms with Apple. I really don't. As I've said, their products are better than great. But it's a slippery slope, one we have to watch carefully. Our culture makes it so easy to be self-involved, and these products simply amplify what the self wants and how quickly the self can get it. This is why we have to be aware. This is why we have to look up from our shiny gadgets and see what's happening around us.

One of my very favorite verses is John 3:30: "He must become greater; I must become less." Indulge me for a second and take a look at the many translations listed below from biblehub.com. I want you to soak in what this verse means:

> *He must become greater; I must become less.* (New International Version, ©2011)
>
> *He must increase, but I must decrease.* (Holman Christian Standard Bible, ©2009)
>
> *He must become greater and greater, and I must become less and less.* (New Living Translation, ©2007)
>
> *He must increase, but I must decrease.* (New American Standard Bible, ©1995)
>
> *He must become more important, but I must become less important.* (International Standard Version, ©2012)
>
> *It is necessary for him to increase and for me to decrease.* (Aramaic Bible in Plain English, ©2010)
>
> *He must increase in importance, while I must decrease in importance.* (GOD'S WORD Translation, ©1995)

He must increase, but I must decrease. (King
    James 2000 Bible, ©2003)

No matter how we say it, the point remains the same:
It's not about me.

Let's take this idea and apply it to experiences within
the church. "Man, I don't really like the music here. I
would like to find a church that plays more contemporary
music." Or maybe it goes more like this, "I don't really
like the programs they offer here. I would like to go to
church where they offer programs I like." Now I want you
to notice something: The reasons listed are not inherently
bad. I get that people like different styles of music, and
it makes sense some programs are more appealing than
others. But let's look at what those kinds of statements
are really saying.

Once you peel back the layers, what those comments
are actually saying is this: The church isn't giving me what
I need so I'm going to look somewhere else. Did you catch
it? Let me say it again: The church isn't giving *me* what I
need so *I'm* going to look somewhere else.

Let's go out on a limb here. What if that kind of thinking changed and the paradigm shifted a bit? What if we
viewed church, not as a service for us, but as an opportunity to serve others? I'm not talking go be a deacon,
Sunday school teacher, or childcare worker. I mean that's
great. Yes, go do that! But what I'm saying is more related
to changing the way we think, changing our mind-set.
What if we altered the way we viewed church? What if
we saw church as a ministry opportunity and a mission
field? What if (now stay with me here), what if we began
to think, "It's not about me . . . even when I'm at church."

CHAPTER FOUR

The Blueprint—
Woman
at the Well

A Samaritan woman goes to the well during the hottest point of the day to avoid what I'm sure would have been certain scrutiny from the other women in town. Otherwise, no one in their right mind would draw water at that time of day. The Samaritan woman knows this and seizes the opportunity to get water without being bothered. Normally, the women would wait until dusk to draw water. This way they could not only get water, but loosen their veils, and chat with one another in the cooler part of the day. (It would be the Samaritan woman's equivalent of today's watercooler.) And we all know about watercoolers. I'm sure this Samaritan woman was the topic of many conversations. Aware of this, and shunned by the town, she braves the heat and draws water alone, where she knows she'll be safe from the sharp tongues and biting words of the other Samaritan women.

Now Jews didn't normally travel on a Samaritan road, but Jesus chose to walk this way anyway. "Now he had to go through Samaria" (John 4:4). Perhaps she was the reason why. Nevertheless, Jesus meets her at that well at that specific time of day, without His disciples.

A Jewish man asks a Samaritan woman for a drink of water. This woman, who may as well have had the letter *A* plastered on her dress like Hester Prynne in *The Scarlet Letter*, understands her low social status in the eyes of a Jew and is stunned that He is requesting water from her. Not only is a man talking to a woman, a major social breech, but a male Jew is talking to a female Samaritan . . . with a past! But I don't think He cared. He saw past all those labels and saw the heart of a human in need of a Savior.

Of course Jesus was aware of her sins. But more important, He was aware of her. He knew who she was and what she needed. He saw past all the labels and aimed to help, not hurt.

He did not trot her out in front of the other women; His disciples weren't even around. It was just the two of them having a real conversation. He didn't embarrass her; He didn't call her to repent; He didn't pray with her. He simply talked to her. He talked openly with her. The environment was real and the conversation was honest. He talked; she listened.

Oh, what a picture! The woman at the well meets the Man who could ensure she never thirsts again.

The water she sneaks to get, the water that is so important to her, Jesus very astutely uses as a metaphor. He speaks *to* her, not at her. He uses something very tangible she can understand and relate to—water. He knows she is thirsty for more than what Jacob's well could ever provide. And she knows it too.

And in her excitement of finding out who He is, she leaves her jar and runs back to town telling everyone she meets about her encounter.

Jesus' awareness of this woman evoked a powerful response in her. She left excited and impassioned. She wanted to share her news with anyone who would listen. And do you know what happened next?

> Many of the Samaritans from that town believed in him because of the woman's testimony. (John 4:39)

The Blueprint Tells Us This

We must seize the opportunities surrounding us. We've got to be aware of others; we've got to look for opportunities to connect.

Take the stories of Rayford, the pastor, and the woman at the well as examples of what happens when we do (or in my case with Rayford, when we don't) have both eyes open. If our eyes are closed, if we are focused on self, we will not see what (or who) is sitting directly in front of us.

What if Jesus had been more concerned with getting a drink of water than interacting with the woman at the well? Would she have left excited? Would there have been anything wonderful to share with others?

Jesus understood the concept: If you want something you've never had, you have to be willing to do something you've never done. By talking with the woman at the well, He broke all kinds of social rules. But that wasn't a concern to Him—Jesus did what He had to do. He had His head up and His eyes open. He was aware of His surroundings and those in it. He saw not just a well, but a woman. And not just a woman but a soul.

Passionate (adjective)
Having, compelled by, or ruled by intense emotion or
strong feeling; fervid

Passion (noun)
Any powerful or compelling emotion or feeling, as love
or hate

> *Nothing great in the world has ever been*
> *accomplished without passion.*
> —GEORG WILHELM FRIEDRICH HEGEL

CHAPTER FIVE

Go Dawgs!

As I've mentioned at least once or twice before, I'm a pretty big Georgia Bulldog fan. Shortly after I graduated from UGA, my wife and I moved to Spartanburg, South Carolina. The town is located about seventy miles from the South Carolina Gamecocks, and about sixty miles from the Clemson Tigers. Although we were only a couple of hours from Georgia, there wasn't a Bulldog in sight, only Gamecocks and Tigers were to be found. On top of that, my three daughters, who are now twenty-six, twenty-three, and twenty, were just babies, so we barely had time to catch a game on TV, let alone attend one in person.

You can just imagine what happened when a guy at my church came up to me and said, "Caz, I've got a couple of tickets to go see Georgia play the Gamecocks in Columbia. You want them?" I was so excited to go home and tell my wife. I said, "Sweetheart, guess what? I've got two free tickets to go see the Dawgs play. Come on, baby, let's go!" Just as the words left my mouth, I looked down at my youngest, over to the other two, and then looked back at my wife and said, "Tell you what, I will go and I will take one with me." She smiled and nodded.

I went to my oldest, Lauren, first. "Wanna go to the football game with Daddy, honey?" She said, "Dad, I'm busy." (She's in third grade . . . and she's busy . . .) Mari Caroline, the baby, was still too young to go with me, so I asked Keighlee, "Wanna go see the Dawgs play?" She said, "Sure," then paused and asked, "What are the dogs?" I said, "I'll explain everything to you." Clearly, I had some prep work to do. So we drove to the Georgia state line where I knew we'd find something with a dawg on it, or at least something black and red. Sure enough, at the Georgia state line there was a Walmart which sold exactly what we were looking for. I dressed my girl up; she was set to go! My wife got all the tailgating food together, we decorated the car, and we were ready for the big day!

Finally, game day arrived. We got up early, got dressed in our red and black, painted our faces, and headed out. We started driving down toward Columbia and began seeing all these big RVs coming in. We saw Gamecock flags, banners, signs . . . it was Gamecock country, for sure! As we were driving in I said, "Now Keighlee, I need to teach you some Bulldog traditions." "Okay, Daddy," she said sweetly. I said, "Give me your toughest bark." She softly grunted, "Arf!" "Baby doll," I said, "I can't take you in there with that. Come on! Give me a real bark, a loud bark. I want you to bark like you mean it!" And out came the best Bulldog bark I've ever heard! I told her to put three of those together in a row, "Woof, Woof, Woof," and we would be set!

So we finally got to where we were going and got all settled into tailgating. We were still surrounded by Gamecock fans, but we were, nevertheless, having the time of our lives. I don't even recall the score of that game. All I remember is my daughter became a Bulldog fan that day, and we created some of the best memories hanging out at her first Georgia game.

About a year later, I got my hands on two tickets to see Georgia and Clemson play at Clemson. Not a bad drive, so I thought I'd grab Keighlee and we'd head down. Just to be sure I checked with Lauren, who was now in the fourth grade, and she said, "Dad, I'm busy." So, it was me and Keighlee again.

We loaded up and started down there. It was the same scenario all over again, except this time everything was orange and purple; there were Tiger paws as far as the eye can see. But I kept my daughter focused. We went over how to bark again (she was even better and louder this time around). When we arrived, we did the tailgating thing and then headed into the stadium with all those screaming fans. But just like before, I don't have any real recollection of who won or how the game went. I just remember barking and laughing with my daughter.

Later that season, I was given two more tickets, but this time the tickets were for a home game against the University of Tennessee. A home game—finally! My daughter and I got all ready for the game the night before. The game started at 1:00 p.m., so we had to get up early and drive. I warned Keighlee this trip was going to take a little longer, so we decided it would be best if she took a blanket and pillow and slept a little in the car on the way down.

We left about 6:30 a.m. and headed to Georgia. When we arrived, I woke up Keighlee. She sat up, looked around, and wiped her sleepy eyes. She said, "Hey, that RV has a big 'G' on the back of it. Listen to that music, Daddy. I know that song!" She looked around some more, sat up a little straighter and said, "Daddy, Daddy, Daddy!" I said, "What, honey?" "All these people are Georgia fans," she said with a big smile. It was then it occurred to me I hadn't told her we were going to a home game. You see, we'd never been to a home game before. We were always the visitors. "Oh honey, this is a home game," I said. "Home games are different because all the Georgia fans are here with us." Keighlee looked at me, looked around a little more, her eyes got bigger and bigger, and then (this is the best part) she held her hands out like Moses, and yelled, "THESE-ARE-MY-PEOPLE!" It was awesome!

I just have to tell you, when you're passionate about something, you want to share it! It's not work; you don't see it as effort. You just do it. And it's interesting what happens. When people are around passion, it's contagious. Others are motivated because of the passion they see in you. Well, my daughter had hardly brought her arms down when our eyes caught these two guys headed our way. These college kids had on orange from head to toe. Their faces were even painted like the Tennessee's checkerboard end zone. As they got closer, I noticed Keighlee was locked in on them. I wondered what she was thinking. Maybe she was thinking about what they were going through, being the only ones there dressed in orange. After all, she knew all about being a visitor. I was so proud of my daughter's compassion for these Volunteer visitors.

Our windows were down, and Keighlee stayed focused on them until they were practically beside our car. I thought, *This is going to be such a great moment for her.* Well, totally unprompted by me, she leaned out of the car window, and as they passed by she shouted, as loud as she could, "Woof, Woof, Woof!" I looked down at my lap, shook my head, and laughed to myself. I have to say a part of me was proud. We still joke about that to this very day!

My daughter was (and is) passionate about the Georgia Bulldogs, just as I am. The experiences she had inspired her passion. I don't think it would have ever happened had she not gone to those games with me, tailgated with the fans (and opponents), saw everyone decked out in their team colors, and heard the roars from fans inside the stadium. You see, once we experience something that resonates with us, it becomes contagious, motivating, and inspiring. It moves us to act. It's almost like we don't have control anymore. We just follow where our passion leads.

When you look up definitions of *passion*, words like "barely controllable" and "intense emotion" are used to describe what passion looks and feels like. I think when we are passionate, we act. We just do—we can't help ourselves. We jump in, get involved, and act. And then that passion in us inspires action in ourselves and in others. It's an incredible domino effect.

I'm not sure if you've heard of the book *Kisses from Katie*, but it's an unbelievable read about this sweet, eighteen-year-old girl who decides to forego college and move to Uganda. Katie Davis took a mission trip to Uganda during her senior year of high school. This trip turned her life upside-down. She was so moved by the people and her experiences that she decided to live there and try to make a difference. Initially, her plan was to go to Uganda, stay a year, and return to normal, American-teenage life. She writes in her book, "But after that year, which I spent in Uganda, returning to 'normal' wasn't possible. I had seen what life was about and I could not pretend I didn't know." Beth Clark, who helped author *Kisses from Katie*, traveled with Katie and watched her interact with the children and people of Uganda. Clark wrote this of Katie in the foreword:

> People who really want to make a difference in the world usually do it, in one way or another. And I've noticed something about people who make a difference in the world: They hold the unshakable conviction that individuals are extremely important, that every life matters. They get excited over one smile. They are willing to feed one stomach, educate one mind, and treat one wound. They aren't determined to revolutionize the world all at once; they're satisfied with small changes. Over time, though, the small changes add up. Sometimes they even transform cities and nations, and yes, the world.

Katie is now the adoptive mother of fourteen little girls, all whom she cares for and teaches daily in the hot sun, on dirt floors. And she does it with a smile because that is exactly where she wants to be, despite the conditions.

At one point, she had to return to the States to help raise money for her foundation and said this of returning to America:

> Most of the people around me expected me to feel relieved to be back. Understandably, many people I saw in my hometown asked the same question: "Isn't life harder in Uganda?" Of course it was harder, in certain ways, but they didn't seem to understand that what was even harder was being back in the States, away from my children. There were days when I felt my soul had been ripped from my body, that my purpose had suddenly been stripped from my being.

She took the dirt floors and hot sun because that's where she wanted to be. It wasn't work to her because her passion had changed her perspective.

This tremendous girl took a trip and was inspired to act. Her passion moved her to make a difference. We have these opportunities all around us, to act and to be involved in change. I wonder why, sometimes, we don't. Why do we do nothing? I think often we try ignoring it, hoping it will go away. We want to get involved but don't know how. Either way, that passion quickly starves and dies.

I think a lot of us feel inspired to act but, sadly, we don't know what to do. It reminds me of a puppy. If you've ever had one, you know what I'm talking about. I mean they tremble when you walk through the front door. They jump, lick, and pant all because of a ball, a bone, a pat on the head, or maybe a two-minute game of fetch. We are a lot like that sometimes: We get excited; we get inspired.

We run around and wag our tails (not literally, just go with me here). We see something or experience something that gets us all fired up. But then we don't really know what to do with it. We don't know where to take it and how to nurture it. And since we don't have any real direction, the passion fades away.

And there are also times we choose to ignore it, especially if it's going to make us uncomfortable, it's unconventional, costs too much, or takes up too much time. I've been moved emotionally before. But then that moment passes and I go back to my busy life. I find myself thinking, *Wow, that story was great; now back to the real world.*

I guess when we stop and think about passion, the question is really this: Do you let it move you to action?

I think it all comes down to what we decide to feed and what we decide to starve. Passion, like most things, will die if it's not fed. Since it's emotionally based, emotionally driven, it will change; the feeling will fade. The emotion has got to become a decision; it's got to become a choice at some point. When passion motivates action, it has the potential to truly impact others.

When we decide to feed our passion by making conscious choices that lead to our passion being fulfilled, that is the point our passion goes from a puppy-dog emotion, "Oh my goodness; I'm so excited! This is a great idea," to a grown-up decision of, "This is what I've got to do, and God willing, this is how I'm going to do it."

If we're not doing something to feed and cultivate our passion, it will fade. But if we're willing to let it move us and take us places we've never been, our passion will grow and will have the chance to impact more and more people. Here's a peek at how Katie looks at it:

> People from my first home say I'm brave. They tell me I'm strong. They pat me on the back and say, "Way to go. Good job." But the truth is, I am not really very brave; I am not really very strong; and I am not doing anything spectacular. I am simply doing what God has called me to do as a person who follows Him. He said to feed His sheep and He said to care for "the least of these," so that's what I'm doing, with the help of a lot of people who make it possible and in the company of those who make my life worth living.

Katie, just a child herself, became aware of her passion and now lives it every single day.

CHAPTER SIX

What's Your Passion?

I believe we don't know what we are passionate about until we experience it and become aware of it on a personal level. I think there is a moment in time when this happens. Perhaps we see or experience something and from that experience a passion is born: a passion for sports, rock climbing, coaching, missions, working with kids, running, whatever it is. But, until we have an experience with it, we will never know that passion exists within us. Keighlee would have never developed a passion for Georgia football had she not gone with me to the games and seen firsthand what it was like to be a Georgia fan. If Katie never took that three-week mission trip to Uganda, she would not be living out her passion today. We will never know what's out there for us until we start looking.

I have this friend who is basically a fitness fanatic. As a matter of fact, she teaches a boot-camp class for our office folks every week. She loves to help people reach goals and really thrives on seeing others do things they never thought they could do. Well, one of her personal passions is running. She loves to run so much she wants others to experience it so they can love it too. (I know. It's crazy, right?) So a few years ago she put together a group of about ten to fifteen people who wanted to train for a 5K. Now most of the runners in the group were not *runners*; many even said things like: "I hate running; it's not for me. I can't do it." But this girl was determined to inspire these people to run. She thought if they could just get over the initial hump; if they could see their true potential, they would be so proud of themselves and might even learn to love it.

The day of the first practice rolled around. I don't know how she got them out there—the people that said, "I hate running"—but they came. Since most of the group was new to running, no one had ever actually run a race before. (No one had ever actually run more than five straight minutes before—true story!) So they started small. They met two times a week and ran a quarter of a mile without stopping (and without throwing up). That's it—that was the goal. The next week they added on a little more, and so on until they were finally up to three and a half miles without stopping. And the ones who said, "Oh no, I can't do it," were doing it. They were running three and a half miles! Their first race was in May; here's what happened the rest of the summer:

- The entire team competed, individually, in four 5Ks (May, June, July, and August).

- Eight children ran their first 5K that summer because their parents started running.
- One member placed 3rd in his age group at the 3rd race.
- Two members placed 2nd in their age groups at the 4th race.
- One member placed first in her age group at the 4th race.
- Four of them went on to run a half-marathon that October.
- One went on to run two more half-marathons the following year.
- One went on to compete in a sprint-distance triathlon that spring.

People who couldn't run five minutes straight, who were breathing hard, hands on knees after running one mile, were doing things they never dreamed possible. And to this very day these people are still running, without a coach, without any prompting or training from outside sources. The sprint-distance triathlon was not the idea of the fitness fanatic. The second half-marathon was none of her doing. Subsequent races and time spent pounding the pavement over the past two years did not happen because my friend told these people to do so. They are running now because they want to. They are running now because they are passionate about it.

None of this would have happened had that girl never said, "Wanna go run with me? Maybe we could train for a 5K together." The invitation to run turned into a passion for many of these people. This passion would have never been realized had someone not been willing to ask and had those people not been willing to try. You see, it works both ways:

- Until we ask, we will never know if they'll come. We could be the one to help ignite their fire.
- Until we try, we will never know if that could be our passion. We could be missing out on something we love all because we never tried.

The outcome is not for us to predict. We just have to be willing to ask and willing to try.

I believe passion is ignited because others inspire and motivate us to act. Maybe they push us out of our comfort zone into something brand new, or maybe they simply challenge us to take our passion deeper and look at it differently. Sometimes this motivation to act comes in the form of doing something brand new, like rock climbing, coaching a team, or running our first 5K. But sometimes this action comes in the form of a paradigm shift, a new way of thinking about what's already there. And often, in order to think differently, we have to peel back a few layers and start asking some questions.

Some of you may be familiar with the *Five Why's* technique. Basically, this method encourages us to ask "Why?" five times to get to the bottom of something. This term was developed by Sakichi Toyoda and was commonly used within the Toyota Motor Corporation.

In the 1950s, Taiichi Ohno, pioneer of the Toyota Production System, would advise his workers to routinely "Ask 'why' five times about every matter." He described this method: "By repeating 'Why' five times, the nature of the problem as well as its solution becomes clear."

This technique has been implemented by many businesses today. If something isn't working correctly in the field, ask why until you get to the answer.

This technique is so useful because far too often the symptoms of a problem are addressed rather than the true, root cause. Because of this, the problem reoccurs. Treating the symptoms may make the problem go away for a while, but until the problem itself is addressed it will only reoccur. Now this technique is great for problem-solving, but it is also equally good for getting to the bottom of something, finding out the real answer to a question. We can even use this tool to help us discover our true passion. I wanted to try out this technique, so I asked one of my very good friends, Hugh, what he was passionate about:

> ME: Tell me something you are passionate about.
>
> HUGH: I'm passionate about reaching inner-city children.
>
> ME: Why are you passionate about inner-city children?
>
> HUGH: Because I think they need help.
>
> ME: Why do you think they need help?
>
> HUGH: Because they often don't have the tools they need to be successful in life.
>
> ME: Why do you think they don't have the tools they need to be successful in life?
>
> HUGH: Because life's different for many of them.
>
> ME: Why do you think life is different for them?

HUGH: Because sometimes they don't get a fair
        shake in life.

ME: Why don't you think they get a fair
        shake in life?

HUGH: Because when I was growing up I lived
        right across the street from some kids
        who had it tough. I saw how they were
        treated. They weren't given the same
        opportunities I was. It made me think
        I'd like to be able to do something
        about that one day.

And that's how we know the whole story. If we
stopped at the first why, we would lack understanding.
But now we know the whole story and have a broader
perspective of what really happened; we have true understanding. Instead of looking at things only from where
we stand, perhaps assuming we already know why, sometimes it's necessary to dig a little deeper and ask why, one
time, five times, even nine times, until we find out what's
really going on.

When I was in high school, actually, I remember
watching my older brother. He was a great athlete. He
played football, basketball, baseball, and ran track. There
wasn't anything he couldn't do. He was Mr. Athlete.

There was a time I wanted to be that kind of athlete.
But I discovered early on I was never going to be the mul-
tisport athlete he was. If I was going to be good at any
sport, I was going to have to focus sooner than he did and
try harder than he ever had to.

My brother eventually went to college on a baseball
scholarship. Baseball was one of the first things I ended up

dropping because I realized I'd never be as good as he was. But the one thing I was pretty good at was basketball. I realized this might be something if I dug in and worked really hard. So I got passionate about it. I practiced; I played. I studied the sport; I studied the players; I learned the game inside and out.

Then, my junior year of high school, I injured my knee. I'd love to say I injured my knee on the basketball court, but I didn't. I injured my knee pole vaulting. (Yes, I said pole vaulting.) The pole actually broke in half; I came down and missed the pad. The good news is my dad thought I was okay to run the next race, so I did. Turns out I broke my kneecap, an injury which caused me to lose most of my junior year.

I was able to come back my senior year, but the loss of a year took the wind out of my sails. I missed a whole year of improving my skills. I missed a whole year of practicing and playing games. I was at a loss because I had this passion for basketball and it seemed as though my journey with the game ended with a pole-vaulting accident. That's why, when I got out of high school, I didn't know what I wanted to do because what I wanted to do was play basketball in college.

I didn't have a great Plan B in place; I had no Plan B in place. I didn't even care what I went to college for; I just wanted to play basketball. But I knew I wouldn't be able to, so I just went to work instead. I was left to kind of wander around for a year or two and figure out my life. Was I supposed to look for something different? I needed to find something new. During that time I thought about two things:

1. What am I passionate about, exactly?
2. How can I utilize my gifts and talents to pursue these passions?

My youth minister at the time came to me two years after being out of high school and said, "Caz, I think you've got all the tools to be a Minister of Recreation." I said, "What's a Minister of Recreation?" He said, "It's like this: You've got a passion for sports. You've got a passion for wanting to see others come to know Christ. Recreation Ministry is really just the combination of the two. We basically use sports to connect with others." I thought, *Great! A combination of the two things I love. What could be better?*

And you know, I had never really thought about that before. After high school, when I couldn't play basketball anymore, I just thought I needed to find something new, a new passion. Never did I think I could use what I already had and take my passion deeper. This aha moment of mine happened because someone encouraged me to look at my passion differently. I knew I had a passion for sports, and I knew I had a passion for Jesus, but I had no idea the two could be combined. In my mind, I played sports—period. I loved Jesus—period. I never saw the connection between the two until my paradigm shifted because someone said, "What would happen if . . ."

I think that happens to so many of us in the church. Often, we know what we are good at in the world, in the workplace, at home, but we don't know what we're good at in the church. If we used our gifts and talents inside the body of Christ we could make a big difference. But like me, many don't even know those gifts and talents can be used inside the church. We are looking for something new, and that may be the answer for some of us, but for many, it's learning to think differently about what we already have.

When we figure out how to use our gifts, talents, and skills to feed our passion, synergy happens. Look at what Dictionary.com says:

> **Synergy** (noun)—The interaction of elements that when combined produce a total effect that is greater than the sum of the individual elements.

The place where talent meets passion is where big things happen. When someone in our office has an incredible talent for computer programming, accounting, or organization, and they use those skills to help meet their bigger passion of seeing kids come to know Christ, that's huge! When you combine gifts and talents with your passion, God-sized things take place!

What Happens When Our Passion Doesn't Make Sense?

Once we find our passion by trying something new or by changing how we view what's already there, we will finally be able to see the potential and we will be able to say: This is exactly what I should be doing and exactly where I should be. Anything else feels wrong. But sometimes, what moves us doesn't always make sense to others. What we love, others just can't wrap their heads around. I'm sure some of you don't understand my passion for football. And I don't understand the reason many people

get fired up about many things. But the lack of understanding from others shouldn't negate the passion we feel
toward Georgia football or Uganda or running.

You know the movie *The Blindside*? Do you remember the part when the mother was eating her $18 salad
with her rich friends? They absolutely did not, could not,
understand why on earth she was letting a poor, black,
teenage boy sleep on her couch. Almost to the point of
mocking, they poked fun at her, made jokes, and asked her
all kinds of questions in attempt to quiet her passion. But
they did not. They only gave it fuel. You see, when you do
finally lock in on your passion, it's the only thing that feels
right, despite what others say. It's like we aren't satisfied
doing anything else. It reminds me of what Katie wrote in
one of her journal entries:

> I spent the day today at the wedding of my friend,
> Lydia. It was a beautiful celebration not only of
> the love two people can have for each other but
> also of the love God has for us. At the reception,
> there was cake and dancing, just as there would
> be at any American wedding. One thing that
> wasn't like an American wedding, however, was
> the congregation of street children at the gate,
> all longing to join the party inside. I immediately
> felt suffocated inside the gates of the extravagant
> party. So for most of the reception you could
> find me outside with the raggedy, dirty street
> children dancing and laughing and cuddling.
> Most people were slightly appalled that I was
> associating with these children—the outcasts of
> society. Many of the fancily-dressed guests at

the wedding even came and told me that I probably shouldn't associate with these children, let
alone kiss them and let them bury their faces in
my hair. "They are street children!" the people
would cry, as if it was some kind of sin, as if
the children could help it. We had so much fun,
though. The children ate up every bit of attention
I could give, danced as close to me as they possibly could, and lavished me with love. We spun
and laughed until we ached and had to collapse
in the grass outside where the reception was taking place. Those who had been shy at first ended
up snuggled close at my side, petting my hair or
kissing my hands. The smallest ones fell asleep in
my lap, despite the blaring music from the wedding. Those who could speak English wanted to
know all about me and thanked me unnecessar-
ily for spending time with them. They were so
happy; I can't describe the new light in their eyes
after all of our dancing.

It's that light.

It's that happiness.

It's that love.

Darling Emily, a little girl from the orphanage, is snuggled against my chest fast asleep, and
I can feel her heart beating against mine.

It's that beat.

It's that warmth.

It's that love.

What Happens When Our Passion Fades?

What if there's not a sweet, beating heart resting on our laps reminding us what's important? This happens to the best of us. Passion is an emotion, so will fade if it's not continually fed. I suppose sometimes we feel like we are feeding it and nurturing it, but in all honesty, we're truly not. Often, we get busy or tired or other, more important things take precedence. What do we do then? How do we get back to that place of passion? How do we recapture the moment?

I will give you five words. (It's really just one word five times.) Why? Why? Why? Why? Why? We ask why five times and see where that takes us. If we do so, we will get to the real reason we are not pursuing our passion any longer. This technique will help us get to the root of why we became passionate in the first place. Once we peel back the layers by asking why five times (or as many as it takes), we will get to that moment in time when our passion was born. We will remind ourselves what that was like, and then, we must begin to feed it all over again.

You see, becoming aware of our passion by trying something new (running our first 5K), or by deepening what we already have by looking at things differently (didn't know I could combine Jesus and basketball) isn't the end goal. These things are great, but they are just the beginning. We have to take all of this a step further and get a game plan in place. If we want this to stick and turn into a choice rather than a fleeting emotion it's important to understand how to utilize our strengths and how to harness our talents. In doing so, we have the opportunity to maximize what we can accomplish when we are willing to let passion inspire us to action. Coupling what we feel passionately about with what we know how to do gives us some real traction. Head and heart knowledge come together and our passion becomes contagious!

So I ask you, what are you passionate about? Is it something you're already doing and you just need to look at it differently? Or maybe it's something you've yet to try?

CHAPTER SEVEN

The Next Step

When we find our passion, couple that with our skills, big things happen!

Well, that's great for those who know exactly what to do, how to do it, and where to go to get it done. But for those who don't, there's a problem. Most of us experience a pause once we find our passion, and sometimes that pause can lead to a complete stall if we're not careful. It's like we are standing there at the edge of something great but we don't have direction on where to go next. We have the fire, we even see the potential, but we don't know how to get from point A to point B.

There's a big question mark staring us in the face. We have a desire, a passion, but we don't know what to do with it. How do we give our passion feet? What's the next step? Do we just go buy a plane ticket to Uganda and find some kids to help? For some of us, we need direction.

POINT A:	The Space	POINT B:
Found My	Between	Big Things
Passion		Happening

The process up to this point fleshes out like this:

1. Examine our own talents and skills to determine what we are good at.

This can be done through self-evaluation, talking with close friends, taking a spiritual gifts test, or even a personality test. Pinpointing our talents, gifts, and skills can give us insight as to what our passion might be.

2. Try something new or look at what we already do in a different light.

Remember the runners who thought running wasn't for them? Remember how it didn't even occur to me that God and sports could intermingle? Trying something new or looking at things differently can help articulate our passion.

3. Find an outlet that utilizes our talents and can facilitate our passion for the glory of God.

Here's where we often get stuck. We've analyzed it, took tests about it, asked friends their thoughts on it, looked at things differently, and even tried new things. And guess what? We found our passion! We know what it is, and we are so excited about it! Now what? What's the next step?

Let's come back to this.

I'm reminded of the parable Jesus told in Matthew 25:14–30. Do you recall the story about a man who left to go on a journey and entrusted his servants with his wealth? They were to presumably care for and tend to his property in his absence. The story is often called The Parable of the Bags of Gold or The Parable of the Talents:

> Again, it will be like a man going on a journey, who called his servants and entrusted his property to them. To one he gave five talents of money, to another two talents, and to another one talent, each according to his ability. Then he went on his journey. The man who had received five talents went at once and put his money to work and gained five more. So also, the one with the two talents gained two more. But the man who had received the one talent went off, dug a hole in the ground and hid his master's money.
>
> After a long time the master of those servants returned and settled accounts with them. The man who had received the five talents brought the other five. "Master," he said, "you entrusted me with five talents. See, I have gained five more."
>
> His master replied, "Well done, good and faithful servant! You have been faithful with a few things; I will put you in charge of many things. Come and share your master's happiness!"
>
> The man with the two talents also came. "Master," he said, "you entrusted me with two talents; see, I have gained two more."
>
> His master replied, "Well done, good and faithful servant! You have been faithful with a few things; I will put you in charge of

many things. Come and share your master's happiness!"

Then the man who had received the one talent came. "Master," he said, "I knew that you are a hard man, harvesting where you have not sown and gathering where you have not scattered seed. So I was afraid and went out and hid your talent in the ground. See, here is what belongs to you."

His master replied, "You wicked, lazy servant! So you knew that I harvest where I have not sown and gather where I have not scattered seed? Well then, you should have put my money on deposit with the bankers, so that when I returned I would have received it back with interest.

"Take the talent from him and give it to the one who has the ten talents. For everyone who has will be given more, and he will have an abundance. Whoever does not have, even what he have will be taken from them. And throw that worthless servant outside, into the darkness, where there will be weeping and gnashing of teeth."

So let's take a look at the first guy. What did he do? He doubled his money—that's what he did! Do you think he did that by sitting at home wondering, *Gee, what should I do? I've been given this money, now what?* He may have wondered for a moment; he may have done some research and looked into some options, but he didn't spend all his time questioning or second-guessing. Once he decided what he was going to do, he did it.

The Bible is unclear on what he did to double his money. I don't think that was the point of the parable. I think the point deals more with the fact he chose to act. He didn't know how the master was going to respond; there was no guarantee. But he chose to try anyway.

Basically, it's the same story with the second guy. He took what he had, used his skills, talents, and possibly even his connections, and earned double.

But as we all know, this is not simply a story about investing wisely and increasing income. Jesus' stories usually didn't revolve around making money for the sake of making money. So I have to assume, then, knowing the character of Jesus, the point to the story is greater than making money. Let's see what happens with the last guy and maybe we will understand more.

The third man, unlike the other two, strikes me as one who is indecisive, maybe lacks direction, perhaps needs to be told precisely what to do, how to do it, and when it should be done. He seems to blame others for his actions, or lack thereof, as is evidenced in his response to the master, "I knew that you are a hard man, harvesting where you have not sown and gathering where you have not scattered seed. So I was afraid and went out and hid your gold in the ground. See, here is what belongs to you."

My character assessments of the third man may or may not be accurate. It's difficult for anyone to say one way or another. But I do think this was true: He was afraid to make a mistake. He was afraid to mess up and potentially let someone down. We can see this when he responded to the master, "I was afraid and went out and hid your gold in the ground."

Has fear of failure, fear of making a mistake, or fear of disappointing someone ever held you back from doing something? Of course it has. It's happened to all of us. Fear gets the best of us and prevents us from perhaps doing God's will, especially if God's will is out of the norm. Or if there's potential to let down those we love and respect.

What if following through on our passion means taking a huge financial risk? Are we afraid then? Sure, it's only natural. But God's way is different, as 2 Timothy 1:7 reminds us: "For the Spirit God gave us does not make us timid, but gives us power, love and self-discipline."

I know what you're probably thinking by now, *Caz, all this is really great. But you still haven't answered the question. What's the next step? (Isn't that the name of this chapter?)*

Well, here's the answer: The next step is the first step. Maybe we can think of it like this: Make that phone call to the homeless shelter to see when you and your kids can serve a meal or help organize their pantry. Talk to your church about going on their next mission trip. Become an Upward Basketball coach and inspire kids to learn about Jesus *and* sports. Lead a Sunday school class. Contact DSS to see what exact steps need to be taken so you can become a child advocate or a foster parent.

There's not a specific answer to the question; it really just takes a step. Do something. I can't blurt out, "Go do X," and expect it to fit every situation. Not everyone has a passion to serve the homeless, so not everyone should make that call. But if you do have that passion, you've got to pick up the phone. Not everyone has a passion to be a basketball coach, but if you do, you've got to contact your church and find an Upward league to serve in today. I guarantee they will have a job for you to do!

Do you remember the movie *Indiana Jones and the Last Crusade*? There's a scene in that movie (some of you know where I'm going with this) where Indiana Jones must cross over a huge chasm—with no visible bridge. Up to this point, he's been following clues from an ancient book in search of the Holy Grail. His search becomes more important and intense because his father is wounded. It is said that whoever drinks from this cup will be healed. So he must find this cup.

Up he walks to the brink, the edge. It appears he can go no further. There is no bridge to carry him across. His father is dying behind him; a chasm is laid out before him. Indiana Jones is left to make a choice, a decision. What does he do? He pauses. Just like we all do. He pauses at the edge so he can decide: something or nothing.

And then you can see it on Indy's face; something clicks. He says, "It's a leap of faith." Then you hear his father whisper, "You must believe, boy, you must believe." Jones's pause was only a pause. It never turned into a stall. He decided to move forward, and he did. And you know how the movie goes. He lifted up his leg, took a deep breath, and stepped out. On faith. And landed. He landed on a bridge that was not visible, initially. Only after he took that first step could he see more clearly where he was going and how he was going to get there.

In his book *Experiencing God*, Henry Blackaby says it well, "You will not get to see the evidence of your obedience until after you obey." You see, the next step is really more general than it is specific. It's more about attitude and frame of mind than anything. Do we see becoming a Sunday school teacher as a daunting task? We know we have a passion for teaching. It's something we've thought about doing for a long time. So how do we stop letting fear make our choices for us? What do we say to ourselves that encourages us to move forward? (Also, equally important to examine is what we say to ourselves that encourages us to stand still.)

Maybe moving forward comes by remembering—and even constantly telling ourselves—we are not in this alone! Through Christ all things are possible. The Bible mentions this a few times:

> He replied, "Because you have so little faith. I tell you the truth, if you have faith as small as a mustard seed, you can say to this mountain, 'Move from here to there' and it will move. Nothing will be impossible for you." (Matt. 17:20)

> Jesus looked at them and said, "With man this is impossible, but with God all things are possible." (Matt. 19:26)

> For nothing is impossible with God." (Luke 1:37)

> I can do everything through him who gives me strength. (Phil. 4:13)

Fear conquers us when we fail to recognize Who it is that is helping us. Do not let the fear of anything stop you from finding an outlet for your passion to thrive.

And I will be honest with you, we may disappoint someone in the process; we may even go in a wrong direction. But then again, we may not. Think of that. We may not! We may succeed more than we ever thought possible. But we will never know until we try. Doing something is always better than doing nothing. If we sit in our fear and do nothing, even the sense of passion will fade and we will be left with less than what we began with.

Jesus concludes this parable with something He said over and over again. (And you have to think, if Jesus said it numerous times, we should probably sit up and pay attention.) He said, "For everyone has will be given more, and he will have an abundance. Whoever does not have, even what he has will be taken from him" (Matt. 25:29; see also Matt. 13:12; Mark 4:25; Luke 8:18; 19:26).

Are we going to bury our bag of gold because of fear and lose what we have and more, or are we going to take the next step, the first step, and see what God can do when we have faith?

CHAPTER EIGHT

The Blueprint—
Peter

Often, our greatest strength is also our greatest weakness. Peter is a true example of that. He's bold, impulsive, and strong. These qualities can be wonderful, when they are in check. Peter was nothing if he wasn't passionate. Often, it was his passion that got him into trouble. But despite his ups and downs, he was the one Jesus chose to build the church on. I think that's key here. But we'll come back to that later. Let's look at the life and character of Peter for a moment:

- Thought he could walk on water (Matt. 14:28–29)
  - Began to sink when he took his eyes off Jesus (Matt. 14:30–31)
- Rebuked Jesus (Matt. 16:22)
  - Corrected by Jesus (Matt.16:23)
- Drew his sword and struck the high priest's servant, cutting off his ear (John 18:10)
  - Instructed to put up his sword (John 18:11)

- Boasted he would never forsake Jesus (Matt. 26:33–35; John 13:37–38)
  - Denied Him three times (Matt. 26:70–75; John 18:17, 25, 27)

Jesus and Peter met on a boat. Peter was fishing and Jesus was speaking to a crowd. The people were gathering in around Him; He needed a boat to stand in. He borrowed Peter's boat and continued teaching to the crowds. After Jesus finished He told Simon, "Put out into deep water, and let down the nets for a catch." Simon answered, "Master, we've worked hard all night and haven't caught anything" (Luke 5:4–5). I can only imagine what he was thinking at this point, *I'm a fisherman. I've been at this all night—seriously?* But out of respect, he said, "Because you say so, I will let down the nets" (Luke 5:5).

Luke 5:6–11 goes on to tell the story:

> When they had done so, they caught such a large number of fish that their nets began to break. So they signaled their partners in the other boat to come and help them, and they came and filled both boats so full that they began to sink.
>
> When Simon Peter saw this, he fell at Jesus' knees and said, "Go away from me, Lord; I am a sinful man!" For he and all his companions were astonished at the catch of fish they had taken, and so were James and John, the sons of Zebedee, Simon's partners.
>
> Then Jesus said to Simon, "Don't be afraid; from now on you will catch men." So they pulled

their boats up on shore, left everything and followed him.

One of the last encounters Peter had with Jesus
occurred in a boat, very similar to the way they met. This
encounter occurred after Jesus had been crucified and
risen from the dead.

> Early in the morning, Jesus stood on the shore,
> but the disciples did not realize that it was Jesus.
> He called out to them, "Friends, haven't you any
> fish?" "No," they answered. He said, "Throw
> your net on the right side of the boat and you
> will find some." When they did, they were
> unable to haul the net in because of the large
> number of fish. Then the disciple whom Jesus
> loved said to Peter, "It is the Lord!" As soon as
> Simon Peter heard him say, "It is the Lord," he
> wrapped his outer garment around him (for he
> had taken it off) and jumped into the water. The
> other disciples followed in the boat, towing the
> net full of fish, for they were not far from shore,
> about a hundred yards. (John 21:4–8)

The Blueprint Tells Us This

From the day they met to one of their last earthly
encounters, Peter surprises us: He speaks out of turn,
walks on water, cuts off ears . . . the list goes on and on. I
have to say when Peter jumped out of the boat and swam
to Jesus there wasn't a lot of thought involved. He clearly

didn't have a great plan in place (considering the boat would have gotten there faster). But that never occurred to Peter, and I think that's what I love. He wanted to see Jesus. That's where the thought ended. His passion carried him right out of the boat and all the way to shore.

As we know, and as is well-documented, Peter's passion got him into trouble on more than one occasion. But also, equally well-documented, is the fact Peter is called the rock. His life changed lives all because he had passion, which at times was barely controllable. Nonetheless, he's called the rock. He's the guy who Jesus said, "On this rock I will build my church" (Matt. 16:18).

A fallible man who was afraid at times, unfaithful at times, and needed correction most of the time, was who Jesus chose to be one of His closest confidants. This makes me think Jesus must have placed a high priority on passion. After all, without passion Peter wouldn't be Peter. I mean, think about it. Take away the time Peter tried to walk on water, or the time he cut off a soldier's ear, or the time he denied Jesus—what are we left with?

Peter was the picture of passion. He showed us how to fall down and how to get right back up. He showed us how to be brave. One fateful day on a boat, Peter was made aware of his passion through an encounter with Jesus Christ. This encounter sparked his awareness and his awareness ignited his passion. He left his boat; he left everything he knew and decided to follow Christ right then and right there.

Without passion what would the church look like? How would it feel—empty, indifferent? Not exactly an enticing picture, is it? Peter without passion would be very similar. The tough and reckless Peter was, in Jesus' eyes, the rock. Not because he was perfect and stable and made all the right choices, but because he allowed his passion to move him to action. His passion gave him a vision to see what Jesus Christ could do if we allow Him.

Vision (noun)
The act of power of sensing with the eyes; sight

Vision (verb)
To envision

> *The only thing worse than being blind is*
> *having sight but no vision.*
> —HELEN KELLER

CHAPTER NINE

The Itch

The greatest feeling in the world is living out your passion and being right where God wants you to be. Have you ever been there? Feels good, doesn't it! You feel at peace. You have a sense of calm. All is well, this is not to say all is easy, but all is well.

Let me ask you: While at the center of God's will, have you ever got an itch? What I mean by that is have you ever felt a sense of restlessness as though maybe your place in His will is shifting? Has it ever seemed as though God's will is moving but you're standing still? Has that ever happened to you?

For me, it happened in the late '80s. I was smack-dab in the middle of God's will. I was at a wonderful church which allowed me the freedom to develop Upward. I was surrounded by encouragement. I had financial, emotional, and spiritual support to help me flesh out Upward as an effective tool to reach the community so children and their families might come to know the Lord.

We were hitting our stride. Our league was going so well, in fact, we maxed out and had to expand. It was busting at the seams. I was in the process of figuring out how we could build a whole other gym to serve more children and families. I was even told another gym wasn't going to be enough—we needed a thousand gyms! Things were going well, to say the least. I felt like I was right where God wanted me to be.

Enter the itch.

Let me fill in the blanks . . .

The first year of Upward, we had 150 players that showed up. I was thrilled! The second year, we had 250, then 350, then 450, then 480. Wow! God was at work. It was great! Once we hit that 480 mark, we had to reconfigure to reach more kids. We said, "Let's have games on Fridays *and* Saturdays, and let's change the layout of the courts. Maybe if we flip them around we can host more games at one time." Well, that year, we were able to serve 520. But by then, we had really gone as far as we could. We had maxed out. We had to put kids on a waiting list—twenty-seven kids to be exact. My wife and I knew that was not God's will for Upward. It was not our goal to have kids on a waiting list. And a man by the name of Dr. Johnny Hunt helped me see this clearly.

Our pastor had asked Dr. Hunt to come speak to our staff and church leadership. This man brought with him a simple, but powerful, philosophy: *Whatever it takes.* He began to talk about the reason we do what we do as church leaders. He asked, "Why do you do what you do in your church every week?" We answered (like good church leaders should), "To reach people for Jesus Christ." Dr. Hunt said, "Hold it. Is there anybody else who can give me a better answer than that?" We were silent. Of course not—that's the reason we do what we do. Dr. Hunt went on, "If you really mean that as a church, as individuals, if you so much as have a young couple that walks through that door, comes in a Sunday school class, and can't find two chairs to sit in, you have just turned away the opportunity to share Christ with that couple. If that couple leaves because they couldn't find seats to sit in, they left and took the opportunity to share Christ with them."

At this point, Dr. Johnny Hunt had my attention. I loved his fire, his passion. I liked his "all-in" perspective. Then, it got personal. He closed with this. He said, "My friends, I have never been to your church. I don't have any idea what kind of programs you have. I don't have any idea what kind of facilities you have. But I will tell you this, if you so much as have a gym in this church and you're turning children away from playing basketball," he said, "you may as well put up a yellow-flashing sign that says, 'Go to hell. We're full.'"

I didn't hear another word. I didn't need to. I got up from my seat, ran to my car, and literally began to weep (not cry, weep). Leslie followed me; we both sat and sobbed over those children. We knew this was not right. We were not going to have a single child on a waiting list, let alone twenty-seven. So the next day we got to work. We figured out how we could turn other parts of our church into gym facilities. My wife and I went to the dining hall. Ceilings were too low; we couldn't use that. Then we checked the youth area. And with the scent of Dr. Pepper and Skittles I remembered this used to be a gym. I went over and pulled up the stained carpet only to find a maple floor! "I bet we can get another two hundred kids in this place!"

I went to talk with our youth minister. He was on board with the idea. He said, "Have at it, man. But I don't have any money in my budget for you. It's gonna have to be all you." He was fine if I tore up his old room. And that's all I needed to hear. I was off to work on my budget. I got all my quotes together, finalized what needed to happen in order for this to work, and met with a godly man in the church to help me work through the details. He had helped me with some other things in the past so I knew he would give good insight.

I sat down with him and told him the Johnny Hunt story. With tears streaming down my face he looked at me and said, "Caz, what do we need to do?" I said, "I need your help. You know that old youth room? We have to rip out that carpet, put down some of that high rebound carpet, paint the whole place, put up goals, and we will be able to reach another two hundred kids! We will never grow out of that gym."

He said, "What do I need to do?" "We go to the recreation committee, go to the deacons, go to the staff, and then take it to the church," I said, rattling off the red-tape steps we had to go through. And he said, "Do you know how much this is going to cost? Have you got your budget together?" I said, "Yes. It's going to be $11,576. He said, "When do you need it?" I sighed and muttered, "Upward registration starts in two weeks. We need it by then." He chuckled at the idea this would be done in two weeks in a Baptist church. I said, "Well, what are we going to do?" He stood up, reached in his back pocket, and pulled out his checkbook. And that man, that man of God, wrote me a check for $11,576 and said, "Let's try it!"

After I picked myself up off the floor, I ran to the church. Do you know how fast you can get through four different committees with a check in hand? In a matter of two weeks we ripped up the carpet, laid down flooring, added goals, painted the place, and were set to go in time for registration. We put those twenty-seven kids on a team free of charge (my wife made sure of that one) and signed up nearly two hundred more!

It sounds like I'm rockin' and rollin' right in the middle of God's will, right? My church is so excited. I am too, but I'm also scared to death because I know the next year is coming. What happens then? So I start thinking . . . *What if we knock down the gym wall and add a whole other gym beside it? We could double what we have. That's another 520 kids!*

So I went and spoke to someone about that. He prepared some plans for me, and I marched those plans right over to my friend's office (the godly man I mentioned before). I told him our predicament again and he said, "Caz, what are we going to do?" I said, "I'm glad you asked," and pulled out the plans. We talked through the details and he asked the same question he did before, "So how much is this going to cost?" I said, "Just 2.3 million dollars. Do you want to borrow my pen?" He laughed at me a little and then paused. (It was the kind of pause that got my attention.) He said, "Caz, you don't need another gym. You need a thousand gyms."

That's when the itch began.

CHAPTER TEN

The Scratch

When you have an itch, what's the only thing you want to do? Scratch, right. So here's what happened . . .

My friend told me I should write a book on Upward and share it with everyone who has a passion for reaching children and their families for Christ. I'm telling you, that motivated me so much I got up, left, and I got on the phone. I called a friend of mine who had a beach house and asked her if I could borrow it for the weekend. I took a couple of my friends down there, and for over three days I talked, and my two friends sat there and typed out every last word I said.

When we finished, we had what is commonly known as *The Upward Basketball Director's Manual*. I didn't know what to do with it but we had it. At that point, I started talking to some of my good friends, Tommy Yessick and John Garner, who worked in the recreation department at LifeWay at the time. I called those guys up and said, "Hey, I got something I want to show you." They read over it and said, "Not only do we think this thing will work, but man, this thing might work all around the world."

Soon after that initial conversation I headed out to LifeWay. I was so excited to sit down with those guys and talk to them about this manual. In the middle of the meeting, in the midst of discussing the possibilities and the what-ifs, someone walked into the room and handed me a note. I was a little taken aback, especially after I read it. The note said, "Mr. McCaslin, you need to call your mother."

I got up and called my mom as fast as I could find a phone. I said, "Mom, what's going on?" She said, "Well, your dad got pulled over by a police officer today for reckless driving." She said, "Don't worry he wasn't drinking or anything, but the officer realized very quickly he was extremely disoriented. Something was going on. We got him to the hospital and did some tests. Bottom line is, son, your dad has a brain tumor."

I loaded up in my car and headed down to Atlanta to see my mama. I arrived late that night. And even though it was late, my mama still managed to meet me at the front door. I went up to her and we just hugged. I said, "Mom, are you okay?" She said, "Son, anything that causes me to pray is a good thing."

Over the next several months, my father had surgery and progressively got worse. And on September 24, 1994, my father went on to be with the Lord. At that time I had been serving on staff at a church. It was an absolutely wonderful church. This church was doing such great things—it was well known, not just in the community but all around. And as some of you know who have served on a church staff, if your church is moving and shaking, there's always going to be other churches calling you saying, "I'd like to talk to you about coming to be on our staff."

Well, when my wife and I were first called to this church nearly ten years earlier, we truly felt the calling. We knew it was exactly where the Lord wanted us to be. You see, when we were first called to First Baptist Church in Spartanburg, South Carolina, I asked the Lord to speak to me through my wife. This was a dream job for me; I'd truly love to have this job. But I didn't want to be swayed by my own desires so I asked God to speak through my wife. I never told her that. I just started praying for her.

When we pulled up that first Sunday morning to meet the pastor, Dr. Alister Walker, we sort of froze in front of this massive church. I looked up at that steeple and said, "Oh boy. That's a whole lot bigger than I am." I looked over at my wife and she was just crying, I mean bawling. I said, "What is it, baby?" (I just knew she was going to tell me to turn around and go back home because this wasn't it.)

I said, "What's wrong?"

She goes, "This is it—this is where we're supposed to be, and I don't want to move but we have to come here. It's what the Lord says."

I said, "But honey, this is bigger than me. I'm not sure about this."

She said, "I know. If it's bigger than you then no matter what happens only He will get the glory."

There was no doubt that's where God wanted us to be. God called me to that church and I was planning on staying at that church *until God released me from it.* There was no need to answer the telephone when other churches called because I knew that's exactly where God wanted me to be.

Well, when my daddy died, on the drive home from Atlanta after his funeral, I started to itch a little. Our roots by now were in Spartanburg. We had been there nearly ten years, but for the first time that tree was shaken. All I could think about was my mama down there all by herself in Atlanta. I wanted to move closer to her. I started wondering, questioning if maybe it was time. But I knew He hadn't released me.

During this time, we were in transition at the church. We had a new pastor, Dr. Don Wilton, and our administrative pastor was very busy trying to get the house in order for this new pastor. That administrator walked into my office one day and said, "Caz, you're doing a great job. I really appreciate all that you're doing. I want you just to keep up the good work. And for the next two years, I don't want you add one thing to what you're doing. Don't add one thing to your budget, and don't add one thing to your plans. I just want you to maintain."

I know and you know it takes all kinds to run and manage the church. There is nothing wrong with people who maintain ministry. We have to keep it going. But that wasn't part of what I knew I had to do. He said, "I want you to maintain." I said, "Yes, sir." He turned around and he walked out the door; I picked up the phone and called Leslie. She answered and I said, "Sweetheart, *I've been released* from First Baptist Church." She said, "Oh my goodness! You got fired?" I laughed and said, "No, honey.

I think God released us. I think the next time the phone rings we're going to be able to answer it." I got home. We talked about it a little bit.

I'm telling you, in a matter of a week I got a phone call. It was from a dear friend of mine, Bryant Wright, at Johnson Ferry Baptist Church. Back when he called, they didn't have recreational facilities; they didn't even have a gym. He wasn't calling about a recreation position; he was asking me if I'd like to be on his staff in a leadership development position. I thought this would be perfect. It would get me closer to my mom. So my wife and I went down to talk. We had a wonderful conversation with him and his wife. Things were moving right along.

We talked back and forth on the phone for several months. He finally said, "Caz, I think we're ready to go ahead and button this thing up." I said, "You've got to be kidding me!" He said, "No, sir. We'd like you to come down here and meet our whole staff. We're going to have a covered dish party at my house. Blue jeans and T-shirts are the rule. Everybody's bringing something to eat. You come to my house, get to know everyone, and tell us your vision for our church." I said, "Man that sounds great!"

It was clear that God was opening doors for us. He was working through circumstances and areas in my life. I had been released from FBC, Spartanburg, and had the potential to move closer to my mom. So you know what I did? I started praying for my wife. "Lord, speak through my wife." Again, I didn't want my desires to cloud my judgment because for me, this was a dream job, a dream church, and I'd be closer to home.

If you've ever been to Johnson Ferry, you know this is a phenomenal place. We were so excited! My wife and I packed up, got in the car, and headed down there to meet everyone. We got checked in the hotel, put on our blue jeans and T-shirts, and were ready to go. I was thinking, *Blue jeans and T-shirts—this is my kind of place! This is going to be great!*

On the way to Bryant's house, I was still praying for my wife. "Lord, just speak through her." Well, we arrived at his house, walked up to the front door, and I knocked. As we waited for him to open the door I looked over at my wife with an excited grin. But I noticed she was crying. So get this: I had just knocked on the door and now my wife is crying. Not good. But then I remembered the last time she cried (the day we pulled up in front of FBC, Spartanburg). So I thought, *Oh, yay. This is it! God is giving us the green light! Yes!*

I said, "What is it, honey?", knowing she was going to say, "This is exactly where God wants us." Instead she said, "This is not it! We have to get out of here." About that time the pastor opens the door and says, "Come in!" I'm thinking, *Seriously?*

So we walked in and had a wonderful dinner. All the while I was thinking, *I've got to talk to the pastor and let him know what's going on.* After dinner I pulled him to the side and said, "Bryant, you're not going to believe this but the Lord just revealed to us we're not supposed to be here." I was so embarrassed, and a little lost for words. But I knew it was the right thing to do.

His response was rather remarkable. He said, "If that's what the Lord said to you, then that's what the Lord is saying to us too." He and his staff prayed for us; then Leslie and I loaded back up in our car and headed home. Johnson Ferry was not it for us.

I knew I had been released from FBC, I knew Johnson Ferry wasn't right, but I didn't know what was. We both left a bit confused.

I got up the next morning, went back into work, and started to second-guess staying there. And I'm not kidding you, the phone rings. It's a church up in Charlotte, North Carolina. They called us and said, "Caz, we want you to come up here and talk to us about a Minister of Recreation position." I'm thinking, *Lord, what in the world? I don't want to go further from my mom. I want to get closer. North Carolina is in the wrong direction. What in the world do you want us to do?* He said, "Maybe you just need to go check it out." I went up there the first time by myself. I went back the second time and brought my wife. We went up the next time, and brought our kids. They were too young to even know what was going on but we just looked around. Everything was falling in place. It was perfect.

Well, the pastor calls me up and says, "We're ready to wrap this thing up." I said, "Great! But what exactly do you mean by that?" He said, "I want you to come up this weekend and I want you to meet our personnel committee right after the eleven o'clock service. We're going to have a vote and after that, it's done. You can resign the following Sunday from your church, give them two weeks, and then you'll be here." I said, "All right. Here we go! This is it, Lord. This is what You want me to do. Even if it means being further from my mom, I know You're up to something so I'm ready to go."

I went home and talked to Leslie and said, "Sweetheart, they just called. They want us to meet the personnel committee. And I was thinking, maybe before we load up and go all the way there, we should have a little prayer time together here, now." (I didn't want a repeat of last time.) "I love it when the Lord speaks to me through you and maybe He'd speak to both of us at the same time *before* we get all the way up there. What do you think?" She came in the den. We got down on our knees, held hands, and began to pray.

We said, "Lord, we truly believe You released us from this church. We truly believe You think our work here is done. Father, this church is calling us to North Carolina. If this is where you want us to go, please reveal to us beyond the shadow of a doubt that You want us to go there. Make it real to us, Lord, so there's no question. And Lord, if You do not want us to go, give us a red flag. Put a big red flag up and say stop, and we will, right in our tracks. In Jesus' name we pray, amen."

I had no more said "Amen" when we heard a knock at the door. We both looked at each other puzzled. "Who in the world is that in the middle of the morning?" All of our kids were at school. So we got up, walked over to the door, opened it up, and there stood one of our dear friends, Lewis White. (He's a local real estate agent.) He said, "Caz, I wasn't sure if you'd be home. I saw your car in the driveway, and I feel a little strange about this but I just wanted to tell you that I've been driving this couple around for the last three weeks. They're looking for a home. I've shown them everything in Spartanburg and they keep coming back to your house but it's not for sale. They've only seen the outside of it, but they really like where it is. They want your house. I just want to know, are you interested in selling your house?" Our jaws dropped.

I looked at my wife and said, "Pack your bags, baby! We're going to Charlotte."

Within ten minutes the couple walked through the house and gave us an offer. A few days later we headed up to Charlotte. We had a wonderful Friday night with the staff and a wonderful Saturday night with the pastor and his wife. We woke up on Sunday morning, went to the early service, and then went to the eleven o'clock service. It was the most incredible service we'd ever seen. We left there, went into the parlor, and waited for the personnel committee. We waited for ten minutes, fifteen minutes, thirty minutes—forty-five minutes went by and then three people walked in.

The pastor came walking in behind, "Caz, Leslie, I'm very sorry to tell you this. I'm extremely embarrassed and I'm a little upset about it but we're going to work it out." I said, "It's okay. What's the problem?" He said, "Well, this being Labor Day weekend, four of our committee members are gone. We only have seven. There aren't enough to make a vote." I said, "No problem. Man, that's okay." He said, "Listen, can you come back on Thursday?" I said, "Sure." We laughed, joked, got in the car, and then cried. I didn't know what in the world to do next.

It was a silent ride back to Spartanburg. We drove for an hour and a half in almost pure silence. We pulled in the driveway. I looked at my wife and asked, "Sweetheart, was that a red flag?" "Yes, I think so," she replied. "What do we do now?" I asked. "Let's play it out through Thursday and see what happens."

Before we left, I told the pastor in North Carolina I was supposed to resign the following Sunday. He said, "You go ahead and resign on Sunday. That's no problem. Everyone has met you; we just have to come together for a vote. It's a formality. We'll see you back here on Thursday." I said, "Okay."

I wrote up my resignation and was set to meet with my pastor on Monday to let him know what was happening. But that meeting got cancelled. (It was actually postponed until the following day.) So Tuesday rolled around. A few minutes before we were set to meet, I was notified Dr. Wilton had an emergency come up so we had to postpone again. It was getting closer to Thursday and I still had yet to speak with my pastor. I was getting a little antsy.

I had already scheduled a meeting on Wednesday with the man who wrote me a check for $11,576 (the same man who looked me in the eye and said, "You don't need a gym, you need a thousand gyms."). I had a meeting with that guy because I didn't want him to hear I was resigning to go to another church from the pulpit. I wanted to tell him face-to-face at his office because he'd had such an impact on my life.

So I met him that Wednesday morning (before I had a chance to tell the pastor). I went in and sat down with him and said, "My friend, I want to share something with you." He said, "What's that?" I told him the whole story about my dad passing away, the blue jean and T-shirt church, and the real estate agent knocking on my door.

I said, "I just want you to know that I really feel like the Lord is calling us to go to Hickory Grove. We think it's going to be great!"

He said, "Caz, do you mind if I ask you a couple of questions first?" I said, "No sir, go ahead." He said, "Are you absolutely sure you've been released from First Baptist Church in Spartanburg?" (He used the word *released*.) I said, "Well, yes sir. As a matter of fact, I have been," and I told him the story.

He said, "Well, I have another question for you. Have you by chance had any red flags with the church in North Carolina?" (He used the term *red flags*.) I said, "Well, yes, sir. As a matter of fact, I've had one red flag." After I told him the whole story, he began to smile a little bit. He said, "Well, do you mind if I ask you another question?" I said, "Go ahead. Shoot." "First of all, my wife and I would hate to see you leave our church. We don't ever want to see you leave because we love you. We promised each other if you ever came to us and told us you were leaving, we'd have to ask you this question." I said, "Well, what question is that?" He said, "If you could do anything in the world, anything at all you think God is calling you to do, what would that be?"

I just started to weep. I said, "You know that answer. You know what we've talked about." He asked, "What would it be?" I said, "I'd be doing Upward all around the world." He said, "If you really want to do Upward all around the world, you'll never have to worry about finances because we want to support you."

I said, "Well sir, that's definitely what I want to do." He stood up out of his chair, stuck his hand out, and said,

"Well then, let's start tomorrow." I stood up, I shook his hand, and I walked right out that door.

I got in my car and thought, *What did that mean? What did I just do? I shook his hand and told him I was going to do Upward all over the world. What am I thinking? We are resigning from FBC and moving to North Carolina. We already have an offer on our house! What in the world am I going to tell my wife?*

I might have had a small panic attack in the car that day once I realized I had to drive home and tell my wife, "Hey babe, new plan . . . again."

Remember, all of this is before cell phones were popular. I couldn't just call my wife. I had to actually drive all the way home (which looking back was probably a good thing—it gave me time to get my thoughts together). It was a Wednesday, which meant Mother's Morning Out for the kiddos, which usually means, Mama is out too. I'm thinking, *She's not going to be there. I'm going have to go find her or wait.*

I pulled into the driveway and her car was there. I walked in the door, and it was one of the scariest moments of my life. All I could hear was my wife crying as though she was hurt; she couldn't even catch her breath. I found her on the kitchen floor balled up.

I ran over to her, sat down on the floor, and I put my arms around her. I said, "Sweetheart, what's wrong?" She caught her breath and said, "We're supposed to resign from our church." I said, "It's alright, honey. We're going to resign." She said, "But we're not supposed to go to that church up in Charlotte, either." I said, "Honey, what do you mean?" She said, "The Lord just revealed to me that we're supposed to do Upward all around this world. And I don't know how I will feed my girls. How are we going to do this?"

I said, "Baby, I've got a story for you." So we sat there on the kitchen floor, and I told her everything that just happened.

Immediately, I called Hickory Grove Baptist Church in Charlotte and spoke to their pastor, Joe Brown. I said, "You're not going to believe this, Pastor." I told him the whole story about my dad and wanting to be closer to my mom. I told him about the church at Johnson Ferry and about going up there to see him, and about the real estate agent knocking on my door, and about the meeting with my friend . . .

And do you know what? The pastor on the other end of the phone said, "Caz, if God had to use your father's death to get your attention and loosen your roots so you would be willing to talk to that church in Johnson Ferry, and be willing to come to North Carolina, and be willing to talk to that godly man to realize God's will for your life—I just want you to know we are sure glad to be a part of God's will today."

After a difficult but wonderful conversation with Dr. Don Wilton, we resigned from our church. I read that letter of resignation to my church family and told that very story (in a much more condensed fashion).

A few weeks later, Upward Unlimited was formed. We had developed a little set of bylaws I took to Columbia. I gave those bylaws to a lady at the office down there and wrote a check for $25.

After about thirty minutes of processing paperwork, she came back to me and said, "There you go. You are the President of Upward Unlimited. You're now incorporated."

I smiled, looked down at the form, and there was the date: September 24, 1995. One year exactly to the day my father went to be with the Lord.

CHAPTER ELEVEN

Not My Vision

There have been many times I make my own plans and then ask God to step in and bless it. But God doesn't need me to tell Him what to do. God makes the plans and we get to be a part of it!

One of my favorite passages states, "Trust in the LORD with all your heart and lean not on your own understanding; in all your ways acknowledge him, and he will make your paths straight" (Prov. 3:5–6).

It's clear to see, through the stories I told you in the last chapter, I needed to be shown, beyond a shadow of a doubt, what to do. I needed to know expanding Upward was God's will for my life.

I wanted to be certain this was not something I merely made up or something I *wanted* to do. I had to know it was God's will, God's vision, and not mine.

He had to put all kinds of things into action in order for me to get the message. Looking back, I think God had me in a holding pattern that year. And it did take almost a

year for all of this to come together, for me to realize God
was calling me to do Upward.

You see, I knew something needed to change; I just
didn't know what. Deep down, I knew I had this passion,
this vision for Upward, but surely that wasn't what God
wanted for me and my family. How would we earn a living? How would I be able to provide for my wife and three
girls?

I thought it was merely my dream, my vision, not
His. But really, it was not my vision, it *was* His! It was
His vision He placed in me. Ephesians 2:10 states it best,
"For we are God's workmanship, created in Christ Jesus
to do good works, which God prepared in advance for us
to do."

He put in me the desire, the passion to do this one
thing, but I wasn't acting on it. I was interviewing with
this church and that church in attempts to do His will. I
was trying to do His will, and yet my wife and I were so
confused. It seemed like we didn't know what to do. To
this day, in my heart of hearts, I don't feel like we bla-
tantly disobeyed God. However, at the same time neither
of us said, "Sure. It makes no sense to us, but if You say
so, we will." We still wanted everything to make sense.
We had no ill intent; we wanted to make the right, most
logical choice.

However, sometimes God doesn't call us to make the
easy choice; He doesn't call us to take the path which
makes the most sense. No, on the contrary; sometimes He
calls us to move mountains. In Matthew 17:20, Jesus said,
"Because you have so little faith. I tell you, the truth, if
you have faith as small as a mustard seed, you can say to

this mountain, 'Move from here to there' and it will move. Nothing will be impossible for you."

This verse is evidence of what happens when our faith in God and the will of God collide. It's the culmination of having confidence in God while seeking to do His will.

Was I lacking in faith? Did I believe in the power of my own faith? Did I believe doing Upward was the will of God? At that point, I'm not sure. Leslie and I were confused. We were trying to remain in God's will and do the exact thing He was calling us to do. I guess the holdup happened because I couldn't imagine that my dream was also God's will. It was so hard for me to think of my little idea as more than a wonderful hobby. And I certainly didn't want to go to the time and expense of creating something that would foster *my* hobby. I knew God had to be the center of it. I knew my vision had to also be God's vision or we would go nowhere—but could Upward be God's vision? At this point, I had some soul-searching to do.

I have this theory: I think when the itch begins and we realize our place in God's will is different than before, we need to listen and go where He tells us to go or do what He tells us to do. Otherwise, we will be tossed around and will end up confused. That's where I was.

God's Word is powerful. When He sends it out, it will not return to Him empty. It will achieve the purpose for which it was sent. God had told me what to do. I just had to believe it. I had to accept it. I had to do it.

Isaiah 55:1–11 states it better than I ever could:

"Come, all you who are thirsty, come to the waters; and you who have no money, come, buy and eat! Come, buy wine and milk without money and without cost. Why spend money on what is not bread, and your labor on what does not satisfy? Listen, listen to me, and eat what is good, and you will delight in the richest of fare. Give ear and come to me; listen, that you may live. I will make an everlasting covenant with you, my faithful love promised to David. See, I have made him a witness to the peoples, a ruler and commander of the peoples. Surely you will summon nations you know not, and nations you do not know will come running to you, because of the LORD your God, the Holy One of Israel, for he has endowed you with splendor."

Seek the LORD while he may be found; call on him while he is near. Let the wicked forsake their ways and the unrighteous their thoughts. Let them turn to the LORD, and he will have mercy on him, and to our God, for he will freely pardon.

For my thoughts are not your thoughts, neither are your ways my ways," declares the LORD. "As the heavens are higher than the earth, so are my ways higher than your ways and my thoughts than your thoughts. As the rain and the snow come down from heaven, and do not return to it without watering the earth and making it bud and flourish, so that it yields seed for the sower and bread for the eater, so is my word that goes out from my mouth: It will not return to me empty, but will accomplish what I desire and achieve the purpose for which I sent it."

If we had gone with my vision, we would have built another gym. I would have simply added on to what was there and possibly been able to reach another five hundred kids, maybe a thousand. Thank goodness it was not my vision.

In 1996, there were around three thousand children who participated in Upward Basketball. Upward was in seven churches at that point. By 1999, there were approximately ninety thousand children involved in the program. And in 2005, we reached one thousand churches (one thousand gyms!). As of 2013, the latest statistics indicate Upward has helped to reach over 4.5 million children and their families. This is not to mention the coaches, referees, and countless other volunteers that have been involved. This, truly, was not my vision.

God placed awareness in me: He showed me how I could use sports to reach children and their families very early in my life. He laid the groundwork with that. My awareness of how I could use sports ignited a passion in me, a passion that led me into recreation ministry. And once I discovered this passion, God's vision was revealed. Now, I had to decide how I was going to live out God's vision. I had to start making some intentional choices, some choices that would change the course I was on. But it was time. It was time to move from imagining what could happen to actually making it happen.

CHAPTER TWELVE

The Blueprint—Paul

Can you even begin to imagine the Bible without Paul? What would the book of Acts or Romans look like? No Galatians or Philippians? The New Testament would be without many of its letters if Paul had never walked the Damascus road that fateful day.

Now we all know how the story of Paul goes:

> A devout Jewish man who persecutes Christians walks down a road in Damascus, is blinded by a light, hears the voice of God, can't see for three days, is miraculously healed, does a complete 180 with his life, and goes on to become one of the central figures of the entire New Testament, next to Jesus Christ Himself.

Wow, that's a mouthful! But before we tie this up and move on, I want to pause for moment and look at where he came from because I think there's something to be learned from that.

Let's get his heritage straight:

- He was a Jew born in Tarsus, the capital city in the Roman province of Cilicia. (Acts 22:3)
- He was a Hebrew born of Hebrews. (Phil. 3:5)
- He considered himself a zealous Pharisee. (Acts 23:6; Phil. 3:5)
- He was thoroughly trained in the law. (Acts 22:3) He persecuted the early followers of Jesus. (Acts 22:20)
- He tried to destroy the newly-forming Christian church. (Acts 8:3)

When we think of Saul today, we don't conjure up positive images. He was cruel to Christians—period. However, when you hear the name Paul, very different thoughts come to mind. Why is that? I think we see Saul and Paul almost as two different characters. But they were not. Paul was all Saul. He carried with him those acts, those thoughts, those ideals, and that strong heritage. Paul was a man with a serious past, a past like few others mentioned in the Bible. So how could a man so steeped in one thing turn and do something so radically different? One word: God.

Paul couldn't have done it! He had way too much baggage. He would have been fighting himself constantly. And honestly, I think he did; I think he fought and struggled with himself on a daily basis. His writings reflect that inner struggle which is why he relied so heavily on the grace of God and on the strength of Jesus Christ. Galatians 2:20 really sums up his struggle to let the old die, "I have been crucified with Christ and I no longer live, but Christ lives in me. The life I live in the body, I live by faith in the Son of God, who loved me and gave himself for me."

Paul never forgot his traditions and all the teachings he had grown to know, love, and firmly abide by. Even though he didn't agree with them anymore, even though he didn't practice them any longer, they were there with him—daily. Paul had to put Saul behind him; Paul even had to put Paul aside and look at everything differently. And I don't mean in a different light or from a different perspective. No. This was radical. It was the opposite of what he had spent years doing. It was completely foreign to him, and I think that's what made him great. It wasn't him. It was God.

And though I'm not excusing him or his actions, I do think his problem was simple: Saul lacked vision. You see, Saul only knew what he knew. He only saw what was in front of his eyes. And like most of us, our perspectives, our ideas, our goals, and our philosophies are all shaped by our experiences. Our vision, therefore, is clouded.

Saul was born a Roman citizen. Not just that, he was well versed in Orthodox Pharisaic Judaism. He was what I would call hard-core! Saul was the type of guy, academically, personally, and otherwise, who would learn the Law, carry out the Law to the letter, and who would protect the Law with whatever means necessary. That said, I don't think Saul was a mean man. I don't think he did what he did out of malice. I know that might sound strange, but hear me out. He truly thought he was doing God's will by protecting it from heretics like the Christians. He saw Christians as a major threat to the Law. This was because the Law was all he knew. That's all his vision would allow him to see . . . at that point.

Saul approached life (like we all do) through his *own* eyes and with his *own* perspective intact. He was shaped by his heritage, his life experiences, and the teachings he underwent as a student. Often, when we enter into situations, we do the best we can with what we know. That's really all we can ask.

Or is it? Sometimes, I think we have to look beyond ourselves. Sometimes we have to use different eyes to see the world. If we constantly look through our own eyes, our view will be clouded by *our* stuff. But seeing the world with Jesus' eyes gives us the ability to see beyond ourselves, our preconceived notions, our fears, and our judgments. We are able to see the big picture because seeing the world with Jesus' eyes gives us true clarity and vision.

Maybe you've read the novel *To Kill a Mockingbird*. It's one of the greats. In chapter 3, Scout has had a bad day at school because of a run-in she had with a teacher. She comes home upset and basically begs her dad to let her quit school and stay home so he could teach her instead (she's in first grade, mind you). He, of course, says no. And then, he gives that little girl some of the best advice ever written in a novel:

> Atticus stood up and walked to the end of the porch. When he completed his examination of the wisteria vine, he strolled back to me.
>
> "First of all," he said, "if you can learn a simple trick, Scout, you'll get along a lot better with all kinds of folks.

"You never really understand a person until you consider things from his point of view."

"Sir?"

"—until you climb into his skin and walk around in it."

Sometimes we have to look beyond ourselves; we have to look beyond how we were raised, beyond our teachings, beyond our heritage, even beyond what's normal to see the big picture. Often that is challenging to do because it forces us to look outside ourselves. And even that's not enough. Sometimes it takes seeing the world through Jesus' eyes, and I mean climbing into His skin and walking around in it, for us to understand. In order to make a 180-degree turn like Paul did, we must see what God sees.

The Blueprint Tells Us This:

Saul did not see the bigger picture; he only knew what was right in front of his face. All he knew was what he had been taught his entire life. He had never been shown anything other than what he had been exposed to growing up. And, as he says in Philippians 3:15–16, "All of us who are mature should take such a view of things. And if on some point you think differently, that too God will make clear to you. Only let us live up to what we have already attained."

He was most certainly living up to what he had already attained. He was fighting a battle he really thought he was supposed to be fighting. And that battle was persecuting Christians. He was not only fighting the battle, he was highly enmeshed in his battle. To him, declaring Jesus was the Messiah was, in effect, saying there was no need for the Law in the lives of the Jews. Saul, who was highly committed to the Law, could not stand for that.

Saul was set up from birth to do exactly what he was doing, He was doing what he was raised to do. And Saul was the type of guy who, when he decided to do something, was going to do it full throttle. There was no halfway for him.

I believe Saul would have continued *protecting* the Law with all his might if not for a vision. He would have continued down the same path and never changed had he not been totally blinded first. I think God had to push a reset button on Saul in order to get his attention and head him in the right direction. And I think God continues to deal with many of us in the very same way.

Once Paul had *a vision* (once he had vision) he looked at life differently. His point of view changed; his vision expanded and he saw the bigger picture, something he had never been able to do before. This big picture, this vision, stirred a need within Paul, a need to follow Christ. From then on, that's what Paul did—whatever Jesus Christ told him to do.

PHASE TWO: ACT

—It's not about me anymore—

*. . . and I no longer live,
but Christ lives in me.*
—GALATIANS 2:20

Introduction

"Do whatever He tells you."
(John 2:5)

—MARY

"They have no more wine," says Mary. Her request Jesus do something about the wine shortage is clear, though unspoken. So why does she mention it? Well, that's precisely the point. She *knows* He can do something about it; she *knows* who He is. But instead of telling Him what to do, instead of invoking *her* will, she merely puts it out there and lets Him decide what to do. Her statement, though not without preference, is open to His will being done.

And once Mary sees Jesus is, in fact, going to do something, she quickly and very clearly instructs the servants, "Whatever He tells you to do, do it."

Jesus said, "Fill these containers with water." As crazy and as strange as that request sounded, they did it. They filled up the barrels with water. Not because it made sense, not because it seemed like the best choice at the time, and certainly not because it was the most obvious thing to do.

What if you knew God was telling you to do something? What would you do?

Obeying God, whatever it is, all begins with a choice, a decision *we* have to make: Are we going to live with intention or not?

In Phase Two we make the transition from *It's all about me* to *It's not about me anymore.* This progression will help us live a life of intention, ready to do whatever He tells us to do.

Ready (adjective)
Completely prepared or in fit condition for immediate action or use

Ready (verb)
To make ready; prepare

> *Getting ready is the secret of success.*
> —HENRY FORD

CHAPTER THIRTEEN

I'm Ready

You've got to be intentional in order to get ready. Things don't just happen. You've got to plan and prioritize and decide you are going to get ready.

Well, not long ago, my niece was getting married. Prior to the wedding, my mother, who was eighty-nine years old, was very excited about attending. She wanted to make sure she got a new dress that was exactly the right color and style for the wedding. So after my sister helped her find that perfect dress, they went to have it altered. They were due at the final alterations just one week prior to the wedding. My sister took her there, they did all the final measurements, and when my mother stepped off the alteration box, she tripped, fell, and fractured her hip.

A day or two before the wedding, I went to the hospital to visit with my mom. The fracture required surgery. Now, I need you to know something about my mama—she is very strong, and she's been through a lot. But as I sat with her in the hospital, it was obvious she was weak. I saw it in her eyes and heard it in her voice. (And though my mama never complained, I knew. You know what I mean?)

As we sat and talked, she took my hand and said to me, "Gregory (that's my actual first name), I don't want you to be upset when I tell you what I'm about to tell you." I said, "Okay, Mama. What is it?" She said, "Son, I'm eighty-nine years old and I just want you to know I'm ready to go home. I've had a wonderful life. You kids, your father—it's all been just wonderful. But I want you to know I'm ready to go home if He's ready to take me."

I sat there, nodded my head, rubbed her hand, and thought how precious my mama was. And before I had the chance to encourage her or really say anything back to her, she continued, "I'm ready to meet Him. I'm ready to go home. But you know what, son? He may not be ready for me. He may have something else for me to do. And if that's the case, I need to know how I can serve Him while I'm still here. Because I'm either going to serve Him or He will take me home. And since it looks like I'm staying here a little longer, I want to know my next assignment."

My mama was either ready to go home or ready to serve. Either way, she was ready! With her, there was no *getting ready to serve Him* mentality; she simply continued to do what she had always done. She constantly looked for opportunities to share, to pray, and to help bring others closer to Christ. To this day, every time I speak to my mama on the phone she says, "Son, let me pray for you." And she does, right then, right there—every single phone call, every single time.

That lady stays ready. She's watchful; she looks out for new ways to serve the Lord. And when one assignment is complete, she is ready for the next!

Staying ready is really the thing we are aiming for here. I mean, sure, some of us have to prepare and get ready. (We will discuss that next.) But I think for a lot of us, we are focused on trying to stay ready; be in the readiness state.

I saw this concept of *staying ready* come to life when my middle daughter was about two years old. We were on vacation at Disney World, having an absolute ball. We were playing at the pool on this huge water slide. Lauren, the oldest, would slide down first. Since Keighlee, the middle one, couldn't swim yet, I would wait at the bottom to catch her. We devised this plan so I would know when to be on the lookout. This is how we did it; this was the rule.

Generally, it would take about ten to fifteen minutes for the girls to make it from the ladder to actually sliding down the slide. And some of you parents may know how these things work: You send your kids up the ladder but can't really see what's happening. You just trust the eighteen-year-old lifeguard will watch out for them.

So Lauren comes down and swims off to the side. She's having a great time! Then here comes Keighlee. She's just giggling. We do this, I don't know, a hundred times. So finally Lauren says, "Guys, I'm getting kinda tired. I'm gonna go sit with Mom." I start to get out of the pool and Keighlee yells, "Wait, Daddy! I wanna do it again but this time I want to go all by myself!" I think, *Okay, she's done this a bunch. I can watch for her and be there to catch her when she comes down.* So I said, "Okay, honey. Let's do this." She was so excited. I still remember watching her run to the ladder.

Well, as you know, these lines take forever. So I swam over to the side to grab a drink of water while she climbed up the ladder and waited her turn in line.

The next thing I know, there's all kinds of commotion at the slide. The lifeguards are blowing their whistles and clearing the pool. My wife and I look at each other like, "What's going on?"

Little did I know how quickly a cute two-year-old wearing an adorable Little Mermaid swimsuit can move through a line when her big sister isn't there to tell her to be polite and wait her turn. Everyone in that line let little Keighlee skip to the very front. She slid down the slide when I had my back turned and went straight to the bottom.

The lifeguard on duty jumped in and pulled her sweet little body off the bottom of the pool.

That lifeguard was alert, and watched every move the whole time he was at his post. I was not. I had been, but not for that moment. I thought I had time to look away; I thought I had time to get ready.

One of my favorite sayings goes something like this: "When the opportunity arises, it's too late to prepare." Isn't that the truth? We can't get ready after the fact. We can't wait until the day of the party to send out invitations. We can't wait until it's show-time to learn our lines. So what do we do? We prepare. And after we've prepared, we stay ready.

You see, my mom wasn't born ready (well, maybe *she* was). But the rest of us aren't. We have to prepare; we have to get ready, and then, we have to stay ready—ready to seize an opportunity, ready to see a need, ready to serve a friend.

My wife is the master of having everything prepared prior to an event. I'm not overstating this. My wife is truly gifted at planning, preparing, thinking of every detail, and then bringing all of those details together in time for a massive event. She does this, obviously, to be ready for the event, but bigger than that, more important than that, she crosses her T's and dots her I's so when it's party time, she can concentrate on the people there, not on the stuff that needs to be done. She plans so she can be present.

Jesus tells us a story about this. It's the story of Mary and Martha in Luke 10:38–42:

> As Jesus and his disciples were on their way, he came to a village where a woman named Martha opened her home to him. She had a sister called Mary, who sat at the Lord's feet listening to what he said. But Martha was distracted by all the preparations that had to be made. She came to him and asked, "Lord, don't you care that my sister has left me to do the work by myself? Tell her to help me!"
>
> "Martha, Martha," the Lord answered, "you are worried and upset about many things, but only one thing is needed. Mary has chosen what is better, and it will not be taken away from her."

I think one of the reasons why Martha was so aggravated was because she wasn't really ready for her guests. She, instead of focusing on them, she focused on her tasks. But, if we prepare ahead of time and are ready, we can focus on people, not things. We can do what's most important and not be worried about all the rest.

I see it like this: You can't *be* ready without *getting* ready.

What I mean by that is at some point, both my mom and that lifeguard had to prepare themselves in order to be in a state of readiness. My mom, at a certain point in her life, had to decide she was going to *get* ready so she could *be* ready, ready to seize any opportunity that came her way. And then that's exactly what she did. She prayed, she read God's Word, she meditated on it, and she surrounded herself with godly people who encouraged her. But in order for her to be ready, she had to get ready, and then, she had to stay ready. To this day, she prays, she reads her Bible, she meditates on it, and she continues to surround herself with godly examples. And, each subsequent day, she makes those same choices again and again. She understands just because she's ready one day does not guarantee she will be ready the next.

I thought I was ready to catch my little Keighlee. After all, I was ready a hundred times before. But the circumstances changed just enough, I turned my back for a second, and bam. Not ready.

See, there's no guarantee the next time, the next need, the next opportunity will be just like the last, and this is why *being ready* is a constant pursuit.

Think about the lifeguard. He, at some point, had to train. He had to understand the protocols and procedures for saving a life. He had to do drills and take tests. He had to practice how to stay alert and he had to practice how to save a life. All of these tests, drills, and practice sessions prepared him to be ready in case the time came when he had to move into action. But here's the kicker, like my mom, this was not something he practiced once and forgot about. "Okay, I'm prepared to save a life. Now I can sit on the sidelines and relax." No. He had to pursue it. He had to be intentional. He had to actively watch every single person every single day in the off chance he would be needed.

My mom and that lifeguard are on watch. They are actively looking for needs and opportunities. But I want to take a few minutes to lift the hood, pull back the curtain, so to speak, and take a real look at what it requires to get there. What kind of planning, preparation, and attention does this involve?

And I can't think of a better example of this than my wife, Leslie, who plans months, even years in advance for something. She is ready for the unexpected, ready to serve, ready to love, and ready to focus on what's most important when the time comes.

CHAPTER FOURTEEN

Who's Coming to Dinner?

My wife does a phenomenal job of planning events. God has truly gifted her with the abilities to anticipate needs, pay attention to details, and plan in advance for the unexpected. For many years, she has taken the responsibility of planning our company Christmas parties. These events occur at the beginning of December and have approximately 180 at one party and about 75 at the other.

I think she and I would both agree early on in our marriage, these big events would become very stressful for the both of us—even though she was the one doing all the planning. But over the years, what my wife has learned, and what she has taught me, is that extensive planning prior to an event leaves room for flexibility, decreases stress, and allows for more time to enjoy.

So to give you an example, by May, the coming year's Christmas party will be basically all planned out. There are still some things to do, but six or seven months out, we are already way ahead of the game. Now, some of you may not think that's a big deal—it's May, it's a big event. (It's really two big events.) That makes sense—plan ahead. Well, let me show you how my wife does it . . .

We were in Target doing a little shopping. She was loading up her buggy with all kinds of different things, but I noticed a theme emerging: Candy Land. (Yep, I'm talking about the board game for kids.) Well, our kids are grown so I asked, "Honey, what are you doing? What's the deal with all this Candy Land stuff?" She said, "Babe, this is for the Christmas party." Now I already know the theme for this coming year's Christmas party—it's a camo Christmas theme. We are playing off the television show *Duck Dynasty*, just trying to make things light and fun for the staff. So in my confusion I asked, "Dear, what does Candy Land have to do with camouflage?" She laughed as though I had made a joke and said, "Honey, this stuff is for *next year's* Christmas party. Since I already know what we are doing, I may as well stock up now while it's on sale for a dollar." I thought, *Who in the world plans that far in advance?*

But the more I thought about it, it started to make sense. I began to understand this was why my wife wasn't stressed out at our Christmas parties. Preparing in advance allows her the ability to sit down and fellowship with our staff and their spouses at these parties.

What's really interesting is when a planner is placed in a procrastinator's world. Someone like my wife, who recognizes the fact that not everyone else is like her, even plans for moments of short notice. She realizes things can happen and circumstances can change, but despite that, she plans to be ready. Let me tell you what I mean.

We got a phone call not too long ago from some dear friends of ours saying the Duggers—yes, *19 Kids and Counting*—were coming through town. They were supposed to stay with some other friends of ours but one of the kids at the host home had gotten sick. The family didn't want to expose so many other children to this virus so they were looking for another place for the Duggers to stay. Now this would be a place where they could have dinner, sleep, and eat breakfast the next morning.

We got this call on Tuesday morning. The Duggers were due in *that night*! If my wife had known the Duggers were coming, nineteen of them on a bus, there would have been months of planning for this special event. Well, I called my wife, told her the news and, as you can imagine, she was a little panic-stricken. She, of course, did not want to miss out on this great opportunity. But, quite understandably, she wasn't sure how she was going to host nineteen people with virtually no notice. But, in the spirit of my wife, she said, "Of course they can come. I'd love to have them."

Had Leslie not been a planner for moments like this, she could not have done it. Had the house been a wreck, had we not had a stockpile of bottled water, sodas, cereals, and paper products for times such as these, she could have never pulled this off with the grace she did. My wife keeps the house open and ready for people. (I guess I've surprised her more than once.) Our girls are still coming and going, so Leslie stays prepared.

She was able to call on friends to help get the food ready and delivered. And, as with most homes, we did not have any place to sleep nineteen people. But, we pulled out sofas, borrowed blow-up mattresses, and made it work. It was one of those things she was able to pull off and then sit back and enjoy because she prepared for the unexpected.

Through all of this, my wife thought it would be a great idea if each child had a special present waiting on them when they arrived. So she contacted a person from our staff and had them gather together large Upward duffel bags filled with Upward T-shirts, jerseys, hats, footballs, pompoms, and other fun things for each of the Dugger children. She wanted all of them to feel welcomed and excited to be there. Well, what she didn't know was the Dugger's friends were coming, too, and they had four children of their own. Leslie did not have bags prepared for these kids and she was devastated (especially when all the kids were opening their fun bags but these four children were not). So the next morning, the Duggers got up and headed out to their speaking engagements. Meanwhile, Leslie began working on getting those kids their bags.

Now, plans had changed a little (wouldn't you know it) and the Duggers were planning on going where they had to go and then coming back to our house for another night. So Leslie had time to gather all the duffel bags for those four children and have them ready that night when they returned. Well, the bags and the Upward items are kept at my office. So Leslie made a few phone calls, got the four bags all packed up, and had our daughter, Lauren, bring them to her.

Leslie had been asked (several days earlier) to go to a matinee with a few friends. She didn't think she could swing it now that we had guests in town, but her friends said, "Come on. Let's go. It will be fun—it will only be a couple of hours at the most. And you could use the break." Well, everything was all set at the house. She had dinner going, beds were ready, even the duffel bags were on their way. So Leslie agreed and headed off to the movies.

Leslie told Lauren to drop the bags off at the movie theater. (Her car would be unlocked so she could just stick the bags in the car.) Well, force of habit, Leslie locks her car. A few minutes later, Lauren shows up. No luck. She can't get in the car and can't get in touch with her mom. By this point, it starts sprinkling, so Lauren thinks, "I'll slide these under the car so they are safe and won't get wet. Mom can just get them after the movie is over. There's nothing extremely valuable in them, so I'm sure it will be fine with her."

Lauren texts Leslie and lets her know.

When the movie is over, the ladies grab their things, start checking their missed calls and texts, and head toward the lobby. They are chatting and having a good time. But when they reach the lobby they notice most all the power is out and the place is practically empty. As they start to walk to the door, a security guard stops them and says, "Everyone stay back."

The ladies look at each other and Leslie asks, "What's going on?" She's a little nervous because she can tell something strange is happening, but also because she will soon have a ton of people at her house.

The guard says, "Ladies. You will have to wait here. There is a potential threat outside." The ladies look at each other again, more nervously than before. Leslie asks, "What, what is it?" He says, "Well, there's been some suspicious bags placed under a car outside and we think it is possible bombs might be in them."

She looks out the window and sees all the cars in the parking lot are gone. The only car left is—you guessed it—Leslie's. After she realizes what is going on, she steps away from the guard to gather her thoughts (and emotions).

Let me make sure you get how big this scene was: There were police cars, bomb-sniffing dogs, and fire trucks—the works! There were people from everywhere.

Well, my embarrassed-doesn't-begin-to-explain-it wife walks back over to the guard and says, "Um, sir. That's my car. Those are my bags." He said, "Those are your bags?" She sheepishly said, "Yes, sir. And there's nothing in there but a bunch of basketballs and T-shirts." He said, "Yes, we know now. We've looked at them. Don't you think it was a bit ridiculous to place duffel bags under a car at a public place, a bit irresponsible, maybe?" She said, "Oh yes, sir. You are absolutely right. I'm so sorry." Then she turned around and nearly died.

I sure hope those four kids enjoyed their duffel bags!

But in all seriousness, this story is riddled with instances of people who were ready, who were on the lookout. The police officers, the guards, the person who reported the suspicious items were all ready. They were on alert and were ready to take action.

The reason they saw what they did was because they were looking for it. I'm not sure, had it been me, I would have even noticed those bags or thought anything strange of seeing them there. But someone did. Someone was paying attention.

CHAPTER FIFTEEN

It's Time

We are never going to feel completely ready to do *whatever* He tells us to do.

Ouch. That hurt a little. But here's the truth of the matter: I don't think there will ever come a time when we sit back and say, "Yep. I've arrived!" If we are actively pursuing God's will, if we are actively preparing, then there will never come a time when we say, "I've arrived." To us, it will always seem as though there is one more thing we *could* do to be *more* ready.

If we look back at the Bible, we will see we are not alone.

- Moses certainly didn't feel equipped and ready to lead the Israelites out of Egypt. Verse after verse, sign after sign, Moses insisted he was not ready and argued with God. In Exodus 4:13, he finally said, "Lord, please send someone else to do it."
- Jeremiah did not feel equipped and ready to speak; he thought he should be older and should take

more time to prepare. In Jeremiah 1:6, he says, "Ah, Sovereign LORD, I do not know how to speak; I am only a child."

- Zechariah questioned the angel because what he said did not make sense. He needed to be told more than once about the impending birth of his son, John. Luke 1:18 says, "Zechariah asked the angel, 'How can I be sure of this? I am an old man and my wife is well along in years.'"
- Jesus said, in Luke 22:42 and Mark 14:36, "Father, if you are willing, take this cup from me."

There are many reasons we never step out when an opportunity arises or a door opens. It could be that fear is holding us back; it could be we are uncertain about what we've been told to do; it could be what we've been told to do doesn't make any logical sense, or perhaps our resources are limited and we can't possibly see how we can manage to do what God is telling us to do, not right now, anyway. We examine our strengths and weaknesses; we look at our abilities; we scrutinize our resources and come to the same conclusions: We can't do it. It's bigger than we are.

Well, *we* can't do it! It *is* bigger than we are! You see, whatever reasons we have—fear, uncertainty, or a lack of resources—all of these reasons *not* to do it discount the ability of God, who, of course, *can* do it.

Wouldn't it be nice if it was more like that "Never Lost" function I always request when I rent cars from Hertz. I love that tool! All you do is punch in the address and it will tell you, "Go left. Go straight. Your destination is five miles ahead." And it's always this nice lady talking to you so kindly. It reminds me of home. "Would you please turn left here?"

And one of my favorite features is that I can be on the phone or I can get distracted and miss my turn and it will say, "Recalculating route. We are going to go straight, turn left, and then turn right. You will be to your destination soon." Man, what a relief!

But here's the best part—I'm getting close to my destination, getting ready to turn into my hotel, and she says it . . . "You have arrived!" Boy, wouldn't that be nice. We don't have to worry about getting lost or getting distracted. The nice lady will take care of us. And, if we follow her directions (or even if we don't) we will arrive to our destination, safe and sound. Well, it doesn't exactly go like that, does it? We are never done. We never truly arrive and feel totally competent and ready because being ready is not a task to be completed, it's an ongoing process.

Let's think about this; let's back up for a second . . . Why are we preparing in the first place? The only reason anyone prepares for anything is because there is the belief that something is going to happen. My wife plans the Christmas party because she believes people are going to show up. A lifeguard trains to save lives because he knows someone could drown. No one plans without believing.

My favorite definition of faith is this: Faith is the belief in something we cannot see is going to happen. Did you catch that? It's the belief that something *is* going to happen. Now, we may not know what that something is, we may have a vision or an idea, but in most cases we don't know in full what all God can and will do. What we do know, what we can control is whether or not we are ready for it. And when we see that opportunity arise, when we see that window open, we jump through it. Not because we are ready, not because we see the whole plan perfectly and it all makes sense. No, we do it because it's time.

You see, there comes a time when we have to act. For a vision to become a reality there must be action. There comes a time we have to step out on faith and obey what God is calling us to do. Do you remember the examples from the Bible at the beginning of this chapter—Moses, Jeremiah, Zechariah, and Jesus? Well, if you remember those stories in their entirety, you will recall each one of those men obeyed. They may have questioned, they may not have understood, some even argued, but they obeyed.

Now I want to make sure we are all on the same page here. With regard to these men, I am not talking about delayed obedience, inferring there was disobedience. What I'm highlighting is these men all walked with God. These were men of God. Jesus is in this grouping of men! These are the kind of men who had real conversations with God, really talked to Him. These men asked questions, they listened, they prodded, and they tried to understand what God was doing. And the most beautiful example of them is, of course, Jesus.

In Mark's gospel, He begins, "Abba, Father, everything is possible for you. Take this cup from me" (14:36). In Luke's account, He says, "Father, if you are willing, take this cup from me" (22:42). And in both instances, the next words out of Jesus' mouth were, "Yet not my will but yours be done." He finishes His sentence. It wasn't the next day; it wasn't later on that night. It was the same breath; the next thing out of His mouth—not what I think, but what You think. Not in My time, but in Yours.

Jesus was in despair, agony (*agonia*—the Greek word used in Luke's account). He was desperately praying, sweating. Luke even says He was sweating drops of blood. This has been thoroughly researched because Dr. Luke is the only one who alludes to this medical condition. According to research (one book in particular, *The Skin: A Clinicopathological Treatise*), in cases of extreme emotional stress, tiny capillaries in the sweat glands can rupture causing blood to intermingle with sweat. This is called hematidrosis or hemohidrosis. Luke 22:44 states, "And being in anguish, he prayed more earnestly, and his sweat was like drops of blood falling to the ground."

Now, I'm not going into this detail to discuss or debate whether or not Jesus sweated blood. To me, Luke conveys the point; the message is that Jesus was in distress. Clearly, in the Garden of Gethsemane, Jesus knew, in full, what He needed to do. And, because He was all man and would literally endure all the physical aspects of the crucifixion, He was heavy with sorrow.

And, this is big, He was lonely. There was no one there who understood. His disciples, the few He took with Him to pray, had fallen asleep. No one but God, His Father, could possibly begin to understand. And that's exactly who He turned to. He talked to Him; He had a conversation with Him. He got real with Him.

"Father, everything is possible for you."

He knew what God could do.

"Yet not my will but yours be done."

He also knew what He had to do.

What God was asking of Jesus was not easy, to say the least, but Jesus knew it was time. And though He dreaded the cup and what it represented, He loved and trusted the hand who gave it to Him—and He obeyed.

See, there is an obedience factor in truly being ready. We can see this exemplified in Jesus Christ. It's twofold, really—the obedience to get ready, to diligently and daily prepare for opportunities. That, in and of itself, is an act of obedience to God. Likewise, the obedience to act when the opportunity presents itself, no matter how difficult or illogical, signifies our love for God and our trust in Him.

In his book *Experiencing God*, Dr. Henry Blackaby writes, "Obedience is the outward expression of your love for God. If you have an obedience problem, you have a love problem. If you love Him, you will obey Him!" It's that simple.

CHAPTER SIXTEEN

The Blueprint—Noah

Genesis 6:9 states, "Noah was a righteous man, blameless among the people of his time." Wow! That's a pretty strong statement. Clearly, Noah was a man after God's own heart. But the people surrounding Noah were wicked and corrupt. The violence they showed toward one another grieved God and "his heart was filled with pain" (v. 6). "But Noah found favor in the eyes of the LORD" (v. 8).

Because Noah had found favor with God, because he walked with God, God gave Noah a vision. And not just any vision, a vision like none other. As we all know, that vision consisted of an ark, a flood, and lots of animals.

Most of the things on that list, in that vision, were not things Noah had ever even seen before. According to historical accounts, it had never rained on earth before this time. So Noah had never seen rain, let alone a flood. Noah had never built an ark, let alone lived on one with hundreds of animals. I bet it would be an understatement to say Noah was probably taken aback by this vision and more than likely a bit confused.

I could only imagine my beautiful bride's expression if I told her, "Honey, let's pack up, grab the girls, and get their husbands. We are going to go live on a boat (not sure for how long) and we're going to wait until it rains. What's rain, you ask? Well, rain is this wet stuff that comes down from the sky. God told me it's supposed to rain and every-thing will be washed away. Oh, and don't forget all the animals. Let's bring those too. We need a male and female of the snake, crocodile, hippo, and . . ."

She would look at me like I had gone insane. Seriously. She would think I had completely lost my mind. "Rain—what is that? A flood—what does that even mean? Live on a boat—how in the world are we supposed to do that? Take all the animals I was with you right up to the part about the animals."

I think we all realize and can appreciate how crazy this idea sounds. Even today an ark sounds nuts! But I think we get that part. I think we understand how crazy this is.

But you know what's interesting? I think God did too. I think God knew He was going to rock the boat (excuse the expression). But did that stop God from putting this momentous thing on Noah's heart? Nope. God knew Noah could handle it; He knew Noah would wrap himself around the idea one way or another. But, more than that, God knew Noah would listen because Noah walked with God. They were tight. And because they were tight, God had an open platform to talk . . . and boy did He talk!

See, God chose Noah. That's big! God chose Noah to do something no one else had ever done before. Noah could have said no. Jonah did. Many people have questioned God; some have flat out told Him no. But Noah walked with God. He was close with God. Noah was ready to hear what God had to say because he walked daily with Him.

Now, I want to pause on that point a moment. . . . You see, when we walk with God, we know His voice, and we understand (on some level) His heart. Therefore, we know when He speaks, right? Well, I've had many people ask, "How do you know it's God telling you to do something?" There's even a book entitled *The Mystery of God's Will* by Charles Swindoll. Books have been written, sermons have been preached, and the idea has been studied. Obviously, this is something we struggle with and want to learn more about. And I agree. I think it's prudent to test what we've been told to see if it's God's will or our will—absolutely! But, if we walk daily with Him, crucify our wants, needs, and timelines, we begin to see the world through His eyes. From that perspective, His will isn't really that confusing, is it?

Hearing His voice, being able to discern His voice is one thing. It, sometimes, is a whole other thing to really understand what He's saying. Just because we hear Him does not also mean we understand Him. Noah, for instance, probably didn't understand every aspect of what God was telling him to do. But did it matter? He still did it because he knew Who said it.

I would love to be like Noah. But those are tough sandals to fill. Now I believe God has blessed each of us with spiritual gifts and talents. For me, I thrive on having conversations with God, envisioning what could happen. But I also like to plan. I want to think things through; I want to talk to experts and really understand what I'm doing before I do it. I think most of us have a little of this quality. We want to see the final drawing before we break ground. Most of us are not comfortable starting on a large project before we know how it's going to turn out. (Oh, I don't know, something big like an ark—450' long, 75' wide, and 45' high.) We want to plan; we want to see the blueprint first. But Noah acted because God spoke. Noah was ready. He was ready to hear God's voice because he walked daily with Him. His agendas, his perspectives were crucified so he could more clearly hear God's voice. And I'm sure God probably wanted Noah to understand what was happening, but I don't think he ever did. Not until he saw, firsthand, the rain, the flood, and the devastation. Quite honestly, I don't think Noah understood *most* of what God told him to do, which, to me, makes this even better. Noah just did it! He knew the voice, and that's all he needed.

My girls, they are grown now, but when they were little we had to continually redirect their behavior. I remember the terrible two's which carried over into the terrible three's (not that the girls misbehaved badly—they really were good girls). But they did have to be reminded how to act, what to say, not to whine, use their manners, and to be good listeners. Now I know if you've ever been a parent, you've heard the question, "Why?" more times that you care to count. Well, my daughters all hit the why-phase at around two or three. Leslie would ask them to do something and they would immediately follow up with, "Why?" (You're smiling because you know what I'm talking about.) Well, then you also know what came after the why, after why, after why, after why. . . . Probably something like, "Because I said so. That's why!"

Maybe that's not great parenting, maybe it is. But when you stop to think about it, isn't that all it should take? Look at it from God's perspective: If we know the voice, if we know Who is speaking, shouldn't we be ready to act? If for no other reason than because He said so. That's why.

Sounds like good plan, but imagine Noah. You are going to see something you have never seen before—rain. And not just rain, but a flood. When I put myself in Noah's place, I think Noah must have been confused. He probably felt like God was speaking a foreign language. And, if you are anything like me, saying yes to something that daunting and confusing would have made me ask why too.

So did Noah understand? Probably not—how could he? But he was ready and he was willing. Noah said yes. Not because he understood; he said yes because he knew who was asking.

Noah embodied what it means to be in that ready-mode all the time. He walked with God daily. He was in tune with God's voice. It's almost like he was waiting; that's how ready he was.

Noah not only stayed in a state of readiness so he could hear God, but once he heard God he, then, *literally* got ready. He built, he organized, he measured, he collected the animals, he gathered his family; he did everything in preparation for something he had never even seen. And though he had no concept of what he was preparing for; he had no idea what was truly in store for him, he did what God told him to do. Not because he understood but because he knew Who spoke.

The Blueprint Tells Us This

We have to be ready on two levels. We have to walk with God daily so we are always in tune with His voice. We are ready to hear when He chooses to talk. Second, we have to be ready to act. We've got to put feet to what we hear. Simply listening but not doing anything about it, is not really listening. If I tell my daughter to clean her room, and she hears me but does nothing, is she really listening? Most parents, like me, would say no.

If God tells us to do something—if we hear His voice and know it's Him—yet choose to do nothing, are we really listening? I think God looks at us the same way we look at our children when they don't truly listen. James 1:22–25 states it well:

> Do not merely listen to the word, and so deceive yourselves. Do what it says. Anyone who listens to the word but does not do what it says is like a man who looks at his face in a mirror and, after looking at himself, goes away and immediately forgets what he looks like. But the man who

looks intently into the perfect law that gives freedom, and continues to do this, not forgetting what he has heard, but doing it—they will be blessed in what he does.

If we are to be truly ready, this must happen on two levels: ready to hear and ready to act.

Intent (noun)
Something that is intended; purpose; design; intention

Intent (adjective)
Determined or resolved; having the mind or will fixed on some goal

Intentional (adjective)
Done with intention or on purpose; intended

> *You don't climb mountains without a team,*
> *you don't climb mountains without being fit,*
> *you don't climb mountains without being*
> *prepared, and you don't climb mountains*
> *without balancing the risks and the rewards.*
> *And you never climb a mountain on*
> *accident—it has to be intentional.*
> —Mark Udall

CHAPTER SEVENTEEN

Are You a Waffle or a Pancake?

My wife loves Hobby Lobby. She can literally spend hours in that store. Some of the time she's shopping, but most of the time she's busy making friends, striking up conversations with people she doesn't even know. Well, she was in there "shopping" a few months ago and, you guessed it, she started up a conversation with one of the sales girls. They started talking about Leslie's boots. "Oh, I love the color. Where did you get them? What size do you wear? Are they comfortable?" You know how it goes. The sales girl went on and on about her boots.

Fast-forward a month or so and Leslie is back at Hobby Lobby. But this time she's on a mission. She specifically goes in and looks for that sales lady. She finds her and asks her to come out to the car. Since they are big buddies now the lady says, "Sure!" Well, Leslie gets her out to the car and gives her a pair of boots just like the ones she wore the day they met. The lady is virtually speechless.

She tries to pay Leslie, but that's not happening. Leslie doesn't want to be paid back. She saw an opportunity, knew it was something she could make happen, so she did—simple as that!

Now you may think, "Oh, how thoughtful. Your wife must be such a good person." Well, yes, it was thoughtful, and yes, she is a good person. But there's so much more to the story. It goes deeper than that.

I want to show you what really took place that day. Let's dig in and see.

Let me start by asking you, was giving the sales girl a new pair of boots intentional or accidental? It was intentional, right? Of course it was; it had to be. No one accidently has a second pair of boots in their car ready to give away. Leslie had to do a few things on purpose and with intent in order to make that happen.

Here's what she had to do:

1. Make a mental note that the sales lady wore a size eight
2. Remember to jot that down in the car, along with her name
3. Call Keighlee (our middle daughter) in Alabama (where Leslie bought the boots) and ask her to pick up another pair
4. Have boots shipped to South Carolina
5. Reimburse daughter for boots and shipping
6. Return to Hobby Lobby
7. Find sales lady and give her boots

None of this was by accident. Every step, every decision was very purposeful. What my wife did was sweet, absolutely. But more than that, it was intentional. She knew she could show love to a perfect stranger by doing two things: (1) listening to what the lady said, and (2) acting on what she heard.

On the surface, a good deed, but underneath, a driving force. See, there's something that fuels that type of behavior. It's a perspective, an attitude, a particular way of seeing the world. At my house we call it seeing through Jesus' eyes. Sometimes we call it being Jesus with skin on.

When my youngest daughter, Mari Caroline, was in high school, she developed a new program at her school in conjunction with Rice Bowls. But before I tell you more, allow me to give you a little background. She had an opportunity to go on a mission trip when she was a sophomore in high school. They went to Nicaragua to help with orphanages. Well, she absolutely fell in love with the people and the place. (*Kisses from Katie* may end up being *Kisses from Mari Caroline* before it's all said and done.) My daughter loved her time there so much she returned the following year. And when she returned home from trip number two, she returned with a burden.

Very clearly, her burden was for children abandoned in orphanages. In particular, she was burdened for children in orphanages who were living in impoverished, foreign countries. More specifically, she had a burden for the children she met at New Life Orphanage in Nicaragua.

Backtracking a little, her sophomore year of high school, she transferred from a public school to a Christian school which gave her so many wonderful opportunities to serve others. (The transfer was something she wanted to do—a choice Mari Caroline made.) Well, her senior year,

she was required to create a yearlong project which could
be presented and, in turn, implemented. It didn't take her
long to come up with an idea: help children in orphanages.

Okay, so we are back to the Rice Bowls project she
implemented at her school.

If you're not familiar, Rice Bowls is a nonprofit organization that distributes rice-bowl-shaped money banks to
churches that collect change to fill these small banks. One
filled bowl feeds one child for one month, and 100 percent
of the money raised goes directly to feed orphaned children in underprivileged countries like Haiti, Rwanda, and
Ethiopia.

Mari Caroline loved the idea of helping these orphanages, but wanted desperately to help the one she worked
with in Nicaragua. So she went to Rice Bowls to see if
this particular orphanage qualified for assistance. After
they researched, they determined it did qualify and would
be accepted as one of the orphanages Rice Bowls could
support. So now all the money she earned would go to
the orphanage she worked with; it would benefit the children she knew and cared for. But bigger than that, other
churches could now begin helping this orphanage too.
Man, did that fuel her passion!

So now she was off to get her school involved. But as
I said, Rice Bowls works with churches, and her school is
not a church. So she petitioned them again to see if more
than just churches could be involved. And because of her
awareness, passion, vision, readiness, and intentionality,
now any organization can come together to collect and
donate money.

During her senior year, she created competitions among the students and even developed a larger bowl so more money could be collected at a time. By the end, her endeavors raised enough money to feed forty-two orphaned children for an entire year!

Just like my wife, Mari Caroline saw an opportunity, knew it was something she could make happen, so she did.

What these two stories have in common is this: intentional action. Wait. Not sure we got that. Let's see them again:

Intentional (adjective): Done with intention or on purpose; intended

Action (noun): An act that one consciously wills and that may be characterized by physical or mental activity

These two stories articulate what it means to look outside self, hear a need or see an opportunity, and then use gifts or talents to act.

Let me say it another way. If Leslie was more concerned with accomplishing her Hobby Lobby agenda than she was with living with intention, she would have never stopped to speak to the lady, never found out what size shoe she wore, and would have never purchased new boots for her. If Mari Caroline hadn't taken it upon herself to raise money, forty-two children would not have had the opportunity to have a nutritious meal for a full year.

I want to make sure I'm clear on something. I'm not trying to focus on *what* we do, *how much* we do, or *how big* we do it. What I want to highlight is the driving force *behind* what we do. For instance, if we act for action's sake, it's only an act. But, if we live with intention, there's no need to try and act. The intention brings out the action in a very natural, sincere way. It works like a sponge. Once a sponge is full of water, the water has no choice but to seep out the sides. Once we are full of Christ and He lives in us, He will shine through us.

In order for intentional action to stick, in order for this to be the natural way we live and think, it has to permeate every aspect of our lives. If we merely try to act, it won't last because it's *us trying* to do a good deed. And good deed or not, we've taken Jesus out of the equation. You see, the driving force is what fuels this whole thing. Without it, without Him, there's only action for the sake of action. And that action, because it's not fueled properly, becomes sporadic or even nonexistent. We may forget to act, or wait until it's a more convenient time. We may get distracted or busy. We, on our own, cannot do it.

"He must become greater; I must become less."
(John 3:30)

I'm sure you've been asked this question many times before, but I will ask again: Are you a waffle or a pancake? Huh? Okay, maybe that's never come up. So let me try this . . . Visualize a big, Belgian waffle with butter covering the top and syrup running down the sides. The butter is glistening off the edges; the aroma of the syrup fills the air. Now look at that waffle, beyond the melted butter and beyond the sweet syrup. What do you see? You see tiny sections. Little squares with walls separating one from the other. You see places where there is butter and places where there is none. One bite will have a whole square full of yummy goodness and the next bite will have none.

Now, close your eyes and imagine a big stack of buttermilk pancakes. Take your knife and coat the top with butter, then pour warm syrup over that butter. What happens? The butter actually melts into the warm syrup—the two become one. Now, every bite has just the right amount of butter and just the right amount of syrup. Perfection! (Great, now I want a pancake.)

But you get what I'm saying, right? Generally speaking, we break life into pieces or sections. We have church-life, work-life, gym-life, family-life, free-time-life, etc. This makes it very difficult for anything to permeate our whole lives because there are walls in the way. And we end up doing this: I will be intentional in work-life today. I will act now. I will do good deed now. Sounds mechanical and robotic, right? That's because it is. It's missing a link; it's missing that driving force.

Jesus is the missing link; He is the driving force. He breaks down those walls because He is everything and He is in everything. I have been crucified with Christ. I no longer live but Christ lives in me—in all of me, in every part of me. There are no walls, no places that have butter and syrup while others have none. I am who I am everywhere I go. There is no work-life, home-life, etc. He is in every part of me. So I am the same wherever I go. It is not me doing works or deeds; it's me learning daily, I have to become less so He can become more. It's not me; it's Him in me.

We are called to be like Him, to let Him shine through us.

- "You are the light of the world. A city on a hill cannot be hidden." (Matt. 5:14)
- "I have been crucified with Christ and I no longer live, but Christ lives in me." (Gal. 2:20)
- "Be imitators of God, therefore, as dearly loved children." (Eph. 5:1)
- "Your attitude should be the same as that of Christ Jesus." (Phil. 2:5)
- "Here there is no Greek or Jew, circumcised or uncircumcised, barbarian, Scythian, slave or free, but Christ is all, and is in all." (Col. 3:11)

Have you ever had an idea or a prodding to do something for someone? Maybe it's something as lighthearted as buying a new pair of boots, or as powerful as feeding an orphaned child. Regardless, have you ever felt the need to act on something? Maybe you saw an opportunity for you to become less so Christ could become more? As I mentioned at the beginning, there were only two things Leslie really had to do. She had to listen and then she had to act, both with intention.

There are people all around us with needs, needs we can meet. Some needs are big and some are small. Some are easy to meet while others take more effort, more time, or maybe even more money. If we listen, we can hear those needs and can see those opportunities. The very thing we need to do will be clear. But it's up to us.

Do we act?

CHAPTER EIGHTEEN

Good Intentions

You've heard the saying, "The road to hell is paved with good intentions," right? (Bet you didn't expect to read something like that in this book, did you?) Well, there's truth to that statement. That's why I decided to include it. It's not to shock anyone; it's to make us think. Sometimes, we have to ask ourselves tough questions and get a little uncomfortable in order to make progress and grow. Much like Solomon puts it in Proverbs 27:17, "As iron sharpens iron, so one man sharpens another." And that's exactly what we are doing here.

Well, when that saying originally popped in my head, I wondered who first said it; I wondered where it came from. And, if you're like me, you want to know where things come from, or at least have a broader context for understanding. So I did a little research and found *The American Heritage New Dictionary of Cultural Literacy, Third Edition*. This is basically a cultural dictionary which breaks down sayings, words, and ideas, both contemporary and classic. So I looked this phrase up and found the best, most accurate definition I could imagine. It said, "Merely intending to do good, without actually doing it, is of no value."

Wow! That's powerful—*is of no value.* But let's think about that: All those times we've imagined what it would be like to help, to serve, or to give. Consider all those times we've had the grandest of intentions but got busy, distracted, or simply forgot. Those times, those thoughts, those intentions, from a realistic and practical perspective, mean nothing.

I should send them a card to let them know I'm thinking of them . . .

I should give money to a special organization . . .

I should offer to help them . . .

I should volunteer my time at a local agency . . .

I should give my friend a call . . .

I should foster a child . . .

I should . . .

Good intentions amount to nothing. I think we should wrap our heads around that concept. It's a bit harsh, I know. It's even overwhelming. But it's the truth. Good intentions make *us* feel good, but what do they really do for the other person? Although we feel kind and generous for thinking of someone else, we, in all reality, have truly done nothing for them. They do not see our thoughts, they cannot feel our inactions. They must see them. We must do them. Let's look at it from their perspective:

> I should send them a card to let them know I'm thinking of them . . .
>> *I never got your card.*

I should give money to a special organization . . .
   We never received your money.

I should offer to help them . . .
   You never offered.

I should volunteer my time at a local agency . . .
   You never arrived to help.

I should give my friend a call . . .
   You never called.

I should foster a child . . .
   You never came to get me.

I should . . .

The other side is very different, isn't it? Good intentions are of no value to anyone but us. They make *us* feel good; they make *us* feel kind. But no one sees them; no one hears them, and no one feels them.

If anything is to ever change—if we are to live like Jesus with skin on—we cannot stop with the intention alone. We must follow through with action.

Operation Christmas Child, or its umbrella organization, Samaritan's Purse, Rice Bowls, Amazima Ministries, and Special Olympics are just a few of the many phenomenal organizations which help others locally and/or globally. I'm sure you're familiar with all these listed and you can rattle off many others as well. Though the mission statements differ among these nonprofits, they all have one thing in common. Let me show you . . .

Operation Christmas Child

samaritanspurse.org/what-we-do/operation-christmas
-child/

History

The concept of Operation Christmas Child began on
October 10, 1990, when Dave and Jill Cooke of Wrexham,
Wales, were watching a broadcast on Romanian orphanages. They asked the question: How can we help the real
victims, the children, who live in these situations day after
day? They knew they could not stop the wars, but they
could offer something—the gift of love. Together, they
filled a convoy of nine trucks with medical supplies, food,
clothing, and Christmas gifts for children, and headed
into Romania, which had recently been devastated by war.
This was the beginning of the world's largest children's
Christmas program.

In 1993, Franklin Graham, International President of
Samaritan's Purse, adopted Operation Christmas Child.
Since then, more than 61 million shoe boxes have been
delivered to hurting children in more than 135 countries.

Samaritan's Purse

samaritanspurse.org

History

*Let my heart be broken with the things that break the
heart of God . . .*

Bob Pierce wrote these now-famous words in his Bible
after visiting suffering children on the Korean island of

Kojedo. This impassioned prayer is what guided him as he founded and led the ministry of Samaritan's Purse in 1970. His mission for this organization—in his own words—was "to meet emergency needs in crisis areas through existing evangelical mission agencies and national churches."

Rice Bowls

ricebowls.org

History

Started in 1980 in Spartanburg, South Carolina, Rice Bowls is a nonprofit organization that seeks to provide food for orphans in the name of Christ. After visiting developing countries and witnessing the ravages of world hunger firsthand, Dr. Alastair Walker decided to develop a proactive means to feed the hungry.

Amazima Ministries

amazima.org

History

Amazima Ministries was founded by Katie Davis in 2008. The organization—based out of Franklin, Tennessee—feeds, educates, and encourages the orphaned, poor, and vulnerable in the country of Uganda. In Luganda, the local language, *amazima* (ah-mah-zee-mah) means "truth." Amazima Ministries desires to reveal the truth of God's unconditional love through Jesus Christ to the people of Uganda.

Special Olympics

specialolympics.org

History

It all began in the 1950s and early 1960s, when Eunice Kennedy Shriver saw how unjustly and unfairly people with intellectual disabilities were treated. She also saw that many children with intellectual disabilities didn't even have a place to play. She decided to take action.

Soon, her vision began to take shape, as she held a summer day camp for young people with intellectual disabilities in her own backyard. The goal was to learn what these children could do in sports and other activities—and not dwell on what they could not do.

Though these organizations differ in their endeavors, all the mission statements have one thing in common: **Someone was moved to take action. And they did.**

Let me be clear on this. There was not a well-trained staff which decided to take on a great cause because resources were available and the time was right. In most cases, it was one person, maybe a couple of people, who were keenly aware of a need, had a deep passion to make a difference, saw a vision of how they could help, were ready to take on consequences (the good, the bad, and the ugly), and then, here's the kicker, they did it! They acted with intention. And that's how organizations like

Special Olympics and Operation Christmas Child came into existence.

Now, I know what you are thinking at this point:

- I can't do something like that.
- Those people were different.
- I don't have those kinds of resources.
- Are you kidding me?
- I've got too much going on right now.
- I don't know how to create a nonprofit.

Maybe starting up a nonprofit isn't your calling. And I'm not saying that's what we all need to run out and do. What I am saying is we can all *do* something. We can all be intentional. And we can start today—right now.

Pick up the phone and make that call you should have made last week. Mail that card you bought but haven't sent yet. Contact that agency you've thought about volunteering at. (I bet they're open right now—go call them—I'll wait.)

The point is we can all *do* something—big or small. It all matters; it all counts. But nothing matters and nothing counts if we fail to act.

And that's really the difference here. That's really what all of this hinges on. It comes down to us taking that first step. And maybe that's one of the reasons so many times we fail to act. We don't want to put ourselves out there and risk being vulnerable. After all, being vulnerable feels so helpless.

I've done some thinking on this, and I'm pretty sure what we fear most can be summed up in *The Three R's.*

These fears, and all they encompass, prevent us from being vulnerable (which means they prevent us from acting).

The Three R's:

- Rejection
- Ridicule
- Responsibility

Rejection: "What if that agency doesn't want me or can't use me? What if I don't have the right skills?"

Ridicule: "What if my coworkers give me a hard time when I try to put on this fund-raiser? What if they don't participate because they think it's a silly idea?"

Responsibility: "What if I take on too much responsibility? What if they want to talk too long when I call them?"

If one of the R's doesn't terrify us, another will. See, I can deal with *responsibility* (I can handle the good, the bad, and the ugly), but please don't reject me. That one really hurts. Or maybe *ridicule* is the one that gets to you. These three R's are all roadblocks which stop us dead in our tracks. But they don't have to.

I'm going to let you in on a little secret, something I remind myself of every day: There is great strength in allowing ourselves to become vulnerable, to become humble. People actually respond very favorably to this (usually because it catches them off guard). Our society does not hold vulnerability, nor humility, in high esteem; therefore, it's almost shocking when someone acts this way. So you better believe people take notice.

See, we don't have to be the best; we don't have to change the world in one day. We just have to put ourselves out there and be available for God to use. We have to become less, making ourselves vulnerable and humble, so He can become more.

Imagine: No Operation Christmas Child? No Special Olympics? What if Eunice Kennedy Shriver never became impassioned? What if she, instead of acting on her passion, tried to dampen it? What if she said, "Not me; someone else should do that" or "Not now; now is not a good time for me."

What if no one took it upon themselves to be Jesus with skin on?

CHAPTER NINETEEN

Jesus with Skin On

Not too long ago, I was traveling back home from a training event and, as always, when I travel, my flight runs through the Atlanta airport. Well, I knew there were going to be problems because the weather was really coming in—lots of thunder storms. And if you travel, you know what that means: delays. As I walked over to see, not if my flight was going to be delayed, but *how* delayed my flight was going to be, I spotted a guy with the longest beard I'd ever seen. He was kicked back in a chair, sunglasses on, and was dressed in camo from head to toe. Mid-step, I paused and thought to myself, "That's either one of the guys from ZZ Top or that's Phil Robertson from *Duck Dynasty*."

Well, you know I can't resist situations like that, so I walked right up to him and said, "You must be Phil." He pulled his sunglasses down his nose, looked over the top of them and said, "Boom, Boom, Boom." I knew with that response I had the right guy. My hunting buddies were going to be so proud! (In case you don't know, *Boom,*

Boom, Boom was the Duck Commander's greeting on the hunting show before *Duck Dynasty* ever came along.)

Phil stood up, shook my hand, and introduced me to Miss Kay. He asked who I was, where I was from, and what I did for a living. I told him a little bit about myself and we talked about Upward. He knew about us and just hugged my neck. We sat and talked for a while. I took some pictures (had to—my buddies would have never believed me), and I headed on back to my seat.

It was about that time another announcement came across the speakers. Our flights had been delayed again due to weather. I knew I had to be home sooner than later because I had responsibilities the next morning at my church. And as I've done in the past, I decided to rent a car and drive home. So that's what I did.

Everyone at our terminal was busy making Plan B. Little did I know, Phil had a speaking engagement at a church that evening in Anderson, South Carolina. As I made my way out to pick up my rental, I overheard Phil and Miss Kay say, "We just need to get a flight back home. We're never going to make it to Anderson in time to speak at that church." I spun myself around and said, "Did I hear you say Anderson? I'm renting a car and driving to Spartanburg. Anderson is right on my way. You are more than welcome to catch a ride with me if you want." Phil looks at Miss Kay and says, "Baby, grab your bag. We are going with Caz."

So I've got the Duck Commander and Miss Kay in my rental all the way to Anderson. (My hunting buddies are gonna love this!) The whole ride Miss Kay, just like she does on the show, started chatting and never stopped. I was laughing—it was great!

While we were driving I got the opportunity to ask him how this all started. Turns out he was an incredible athlete in school, and was also very smart. He attended Louisiana Tech University on a football scholarship and became the starting quarterback for the football team. Well, Miss Kay had fallen in love with him while they were in school, but apparently he was always getting into trouble. She just kept working on him and finally got him to come to church. And when he did, he became a believer. He was sold out.

Okay, so not only was he the starting quarterback, but Terry Bradshaw was his backup. And Terry would always ride him about getting serious about playing football. Phil would come late to practice, wouldn't work out; it was pretty clear he wasn't into it. And so Terry would stay on him. One day the two had a conversation and Phil asked, "You're really into this football stuff, aren't you?" Terry said, "Yes, it's my whole life." Phil replied, "Terry, you take the bucks, and I'll take the ducks." And with that, Phil quit playing football.

Not too long after, he and Miss Kay were married. She was working for an executive at the time. Her boss came to her and said, "we need someone to lead our group on a duck hunt." She told him her husband is the best, so her boss said, "Okay, great. He's hired."

So here goes Phil and a bunch of executives on a hunting trip. They got more ducks than ever before. Her boss raved about the duck calls. He said, "Son, you can make a lot of money with those things." Phil laughed and said,

"You gotta have money to make money." The executive asked, "How much do you need?" Phil said, "About $30K." "Well, okay. When you make your money, just pay me back."

One thing leads to another, next thing Phil knows he's speaking at a Ducks Unlimited conference. He has them rolling in the aisles. His time is up so he hands it over to the emcee and heads back to his seat. But apparently he's not finished. The emcee gets him back up on stage to do more. Phil asks, "What do you want me to talk about now?" The guy says, "You're doing a great job! They love you! Talk about whatever you want. You've got ten more minutes." Phil pauses, looks at Miss Kay and says, "Baby, hand me my Bible."

Phil got back up on stage and began to share Jesus with those men and women in that room. He's been preaching at churches ever since. About a week after that conference, Ducks Unlimited called him and asked if he would speak again the following year. They told him what a wonderful job he did and how much everyone loved him. So Phil said sure. The man on the other end said, "Great. Just keep in mind, you can't talk about Jesus." Phil said, "Wait. Then no thanks. I'm not interested."

Thirty minutes later the president of Ducks Unlimited called Phil back and said that they would love to have him; he could talk about anything he wanted. And Phil said, "Okay. I'll be there."

This man used duck calls, something as unconventional as calling in ducks, as a platform to reach others. Somehow he was able to go from teaching these men duck calls to sharing the love of Jesus. That is a direct result of a man who saw an opportunity and seized it. He went for it. He became Jesus with skin on to those folks, right then and right there. (He became Jesus in camo to those men, and there's not a single thing wrong with that.)

You see, he can reach people I can't. With his unique gifts and talents comes a unique platform. One I don't have. But, I've got my own, and so do you. When he was called back up on stage to talk for ten more minutes, I'm sure they weren't thinking he would preach. I bet that was the furthest thing from their minds. But it wasn't for him. For Phil, it was the clear choice, the obvious thing to do. He wasn't concerned about how'd they react to him. (Would they reject him or ridicule him?) He just did it because that's what came natural to him. And, like a sponge that overflows with what's inside, Phil's other passion poured out onto those men and they hung on his every word.

This story leads me to consider two things:

1. Phil took advantage of an opportunity presented to him.
2. Talking about Jesus was natural for him.

Let's look at the first one. He took advantage of an opportunity presented to him. He could have said or done anything and would have had a captive audience. He could have made them laugh, or taught them more duck calls. Instead, he chose, with intention, to talk about Jesus. He was aware of the platform he'd been given and he saw a chance to share his passion with others, so he did.

Phil did not arrive at the Ducks Unlimited conference with a plan to preach. Which brings me to the second part of this: He just did what came natural. Let me ask you, if Phil lived life compartmentalized, if he lived life in sections, work-life, home-life, church-life, would he have been able to do that? Would he have been able to flip the switch? After all, he was inundated in his work-life at that point. So I highly doubt he would have been able to turn one off and turn another on, especially given those circumstances.

See, those waffle-walls we build keep God from permeating every aspect of our lives. Unless we are in church-mode, He's not coming out—He's trapped behind a wall. Everything, every part of who we are has to be in sync. And in doing this, we are actually able to relax. Instead of trying to *think to act*, we just act. It's not because we *must or should*, it's just who we are.

I think once we get past our fears and recognize the Three R's when we see them, we can move forward. Initially, it might be helpful to use a checklist of sorts to help us break down waffle-walls and transform into true doers of His Word. Then, once we break down those walls and allow Christ to live in us, we will no longer need a list. It will be natural—like a sponge—whatever's inside is what will come out.

So here's that list to get us going. But remember, this is just to get us started. We, eventually, need to get to the point where these things become natural:

1. Be aware.
2. Have passion.
3. See a vision.
4. Get ready.
5. Live with intention.

1. Be aware. What this really means is we are not focused on self. We can choose to live one of two ways: We can focus on self or we can focus on others. That's it—it's pretty much black and white. If we are aware of others, look after their needs, and seek to build them up, we will not be so focused on ourselves. (It's the law of replacement.) In addition to replacing *us* with *them*, another interesting thing takes place: We begin to pick up on needs, expressions, and social cues which lead us to serve with precision. We begin to get really good at noticing when someone could use a hand or a kind word. The more we do it, the better we get. Awareness breeds awareness. And, in most cases, once that sense of awareness has been developed it leads to passion.

2. Have passion. Everyone has a passion for something—big or small. It doesn't have to be for children in Uganda. It can be hospitality, loving on others, or simply making people feel good. It can be anything. I think most all of us have a passion for something, or did at one time. We, over the years, have maybe become a bit jaded. Or maybe we just got busy. Nonetheless, we choose to do nothing to foster our passion. And so what happens? Our passion fades and eventually dies.

Passion is much akin to a plant or a flower. If we don't take care of it; if we don't prune it, water it, give it sunlight, and give it food, the plant won't survive. And for some of us, it's easier that way. We will never be called to invest, financially or emotionally; we will never be held accountable; we will never let anyone down. It's easier this way. I understand. Living out your passion is hard. Sometimes it hurts. But every time, it's worth it.

3. See a vision. The word *vision* does not mean something elusive or mysterious. What I'm talking about here is very practical. In this case, having a vision really means seeing the possibility or the potential our actions could have on others. "I wonder how many people I could help if I raise money for Rice Bowls. How would that pan out?" Well, for starters, the money provides food for hungry children. So because of a vision, hungry children will have food. Maybe others see this and they get involved too. Perhaps they decide to collect money for Rice Bowls at their church or in their workplace.

We imagine how our actions might have a domino effect.

We never know precisely how our actions will impact others, but we can dream; we can imagine. In our minds, we can see those dominos falling over, one-by-one. All it takes is one thought, one question: "What if?"

4. Get ready. As we discussed in the *Readiness* section, this concept means we have intentionally decided to pay attention. We have done our due diligence, and can serve at a moment's notice. In this, we may not ever feel ready, but we are as ready as ready can be. We have our head up; we have been made aware of those around us; we have a passion for them, a vision for them, and we are ready for them.

As you may recall, this sense of being ready is twofold: ready to hear and ready to act. We are ready to accept whatever comes our way (the responsibility, the ridicule, or the rejection). Likewise, we are ready to do; ready to obey.

5. Live with intention. In this section, we discuss putting feet to our thoughts. Instead of thinking, *I should have*, we actually do. How many times have I asked myself why I didn't say something sooner to my friend Rayford? Why didn't I tell him how important Jesus Christ was to me? He was my best friend . . . *I should have* . . .

We all live with those regrets.

But part of being intentional means living life without regret. Instead of thinking about all the times *we should have* done something, we do them. Simply having good intentions is not enough. Being aware isn't enough, and being ready isn't enough. We have to act.

Without awareness, we wouldn't have passion. Without passion, we would lack vision, and without vision we would never decide to get ready. But without action, without being deliberate, nothing happens. Nothing.

This checklist can serve as a daily reminder. It can help guide us through the stages we undergo so we can transform from being self-focused to others-focused.

I don't know about you, but I want to lead an intentional life. I want my time on this planet to matter. And when I arrive in heaven, I want my Father to look at me and say, "Well done, good and faithful servant" (Matt. 25:21).

CHAPTER TWENTY

The Blueprint— Jesus

As you've been reading this book, perhaps you've noticed each section concludes with a chapter entitled, *The Blueprint*. These chapters offer biblical examples for us to examine, learn from, and even imitate. In the section on *Awareness*, we talked about the woman at the well. In the section about *Passion*, we discussed Peter. Paul taught us about *Vision*, and Noah was the picture of *Readiness*.

As we approach the finish line with *Intentionality*, I know of no better blueprint to examine than Jesus Christ Himself. He truly lived an intentional life.

Jesus embodied all the qualities we've discussed. Not only was He aware, passionate, a visionary, and ready, but He actually implemented these things on a daily basis. He walked the talk; He practiced what He preached.

But here's something that makes this truly remarkable: Jesus not only embodied these traits, but He influenced others to do the same.

Jesus was aware, and He caused others to be aware. Not only did He live a passionate life Himself, but His actions evoked passion in others. He, most assuredly, had a vision, but He never wanted to stop with *His* vision because part of *His* vision was to cast it to others. Jesus was ready, and others followed suit. Often, they didn't know what they were preparing for or why, but Jesus said to, so they did.

And this brings us to intentionality. Jesus was the ultimate example of this. He never stopped short. He carried out the task. He did what He was sent to do, even if that meant death. And as followers of Christ, we are asked to live as He did, to live an intentional life.

Jesus

Let's begin by looking at the backdrop, or the point of reference Jesus used for every action and decision He made. Really, what we are doing here is examining what colored His life.

Let's go directly to His Word. What better place to learn more about Him:

> "I tell you the truth, the Son can do nothing by himself; he can only do what he sees his Father doing, because whatever the Father does the Son also does." (John 5:19)

> "By myself I can do nothing; . . . for I seek not to please myself but him who sent me." (John 5:30)

These verses are just a couple which serve to highlight the essence of Jesus. It wasn't about Him. He didn't live to see what He could accumulate or how happy he could make Himself. And that will be our starting point.

Jesus and His Disciples

I think we can learn more about Jesus, more about the overarching theme of His life, by looking at some of the major decisions He made while on earth. Choosing to have disciples, and choosing precisely which ones to have are among some of the most critical choices He made.

Jesus handpicked these guys, one-by-one, even Judas. Jesus carefully, and with great intention, sought out each man with the purpose of making him a disciple of Christ.

Now Jesus didn't choose men He liked to hang out with. (He may have liked hanging out with them, but that wasn't His motivation.) He didn't choose the ones He had the most in common with, and He didn't choose them based on how they looked or how they dressed.

Before we examine *why* He chose these individual men, I would like to look at why He chose to have disciples in the first place. Clearly, it was to create a lineage. He taught them so they could in turn teach others. After all, His last commandment to them was:

> "Therefore go and make disciples of all nations, baptizing them in the name of the Father and of the Son and of the Holy Spirit, and teaching them to obey everything I have commanded you. And surely I am with you always, to the very end of the age." (Matt. 28:19–20)

Jesus knew His time with the disciples was critical. He knew He had to prepare them to be without Him and to withstand what came along with that. Jesus spent three years with these men, taking every opportunity to teach them and correct them. Sometimes they understood, and sometimes they did not. But Jesus never seemed to tire of teaching the same concepts over and over in differing ways so each of them would understand.

We are pretty certain we know why Jesus made the choice to have disciples—to further His kingdom after He was gone. But why did He choose these guys specifically?

I don't know exactly why He chose Peter, Mark, or Matthew. But I do think Jesus wanted to reach as many as possible, so He chose men we could relate to. I think He chose men who, from a socioeconomic perspective, to profession, to personality, possess traits and characteristics similar to the ones you and I have. Although they are different from one another, they are all relatable to us.

Since these men differ from one another, yet are relatable, we are able to see how Jesus interacts with a wide array of personalities, strengths, and weaknesses. Even though the men are different, and at times Jesus' way of dealing with them is different, the message He conveys stays the same.

The style and theme of each of the Gospels reflect their distinct temperaments. And I bet if we ask ten different people what their favorite Gospel is, we would hear different answers every time. It's because people, based on their unique experiences, see, hear, and read things differently. What resonates with one person might not with another. One person may need to hear about love as seen through

John's eyes, while someone else may need to hear about mercy as seen through Luke's eyes.

Jesus not only taught them so they could understand and tell others, He intentionally chose different men with differing experiences so they would, in turn, teach differently. This philosophy broadens the scope of who they are able to reach.

Paul figured that out. Paul saw how Jesus lived, how He was able to reach so many different people, and he duplicated that, as is evidenced in 1 Corinthians 9:19–22:

> Though I am free and belong to no man, I make myself a slave to everyone, to win as many as possible. To the Jews I became like a Jew, to win the Jews. To those under the law I became like one under the law (though I myself am not under the law), so as to win those under the law. To those not having the law I became like one not having the law (though I am not free from God's law but am under Christ's law), so as to win those not having the law. To the weak I became weak, to win the weak. I have become all things to all people so that by all possible means I might save some.

Every aspect of how Jesus interacted with His disciples was intentional, from the beginning to the end. Every last thing He did with them and for them had meaning, purpose, and was fueled by intention.

One of the greatest intentional acts Jesus performed for His disciples was when He washed their feet. To this day I have to wrap my head around that one.

Before we delve in, I want to take a quick detour and point out the fact this story is found in the book of John. I think that's noteworthy because it supports what we've been talking about.

John's gospel is a different account than the others: the style, the feel, and the symbolism. Bible scholars have even lumped Matthew, Mark, and Luke together, calling them the Synoptic Gospels, while John is not included. His is different. And I think there's a reason for that.

It's different because he was different. He looked at things uniquely; his perspective was not the same as the others. The Synoptic Gospels have similar points of view and seem to tell the same stories, albeit from varying perspectives, but nonetheless, similar accounts. John stands out.

Now I don't know if Jesus favored John or not. The point, though, is that John seems to think He did. Five times in his Gospel he calls himself the *disciple whom Jesus loved*. But nowhere else is that found. So does Jesus love John more? Is that what John even meant?

Who knows—my guess would be no; Jesus did not favor John. Beyond that, I don't think that's what John meant in the first place. I think John realized the greatness of Jesus Christ; John had immense respect for His authority. Likewise, John recognized the position of man and the need man had (has) for a Savior. As is reflected in his writings, John seems to understand the vast love God has for His people; he understands what that truly involves, not just on the part of man, but also on the part of God:

- "For God so loved the world that he gave his one and only Son, that whoever believes in him shall not perish but have eternal life." (John 3:16)

- "He must become greater; I must become less." (John 3:30)
- "As the Father has loved me, so I have loved you. Now remain in my love. If you obey my commands, you will remain in my love, just as I have obeyed my Father's commands and remain in his love." (John 15:9–10)

Everything he writes about, even his style and his voice, center on love. In subsequent books, he continues with this theme. His immense love and respect for Jesus Christ was his backdrop, so when he wrote, that's what came out. And that might be the very reason the story of Jesus washing the disciples' feet is in John's account.

Okay, back to Jesus.

I think when most people hear the story about Jesus washing the disciples' feet, feelings of awe arise. It's almost hard to imagine this taking place. I guess it's the image we conjure up of Jesus on His hands and knees washing the dirty feet of His chosen that makes us uncomfortable.

But you know what? As I sit and write this, something occurs to me: Why is this act so hard for us to wrap our heads around? Is it the humility it required? Is it the way He made Himself so vulnerable? I bet most of us want to yell like Peter and insist, "You should not be doing this! You will not wash my feet!" What is it that makes us shake our heads? What is it about this picture that makes us so uncomfortable?

I think the answer can be found in who Jesus was and what His perspective on life was all about. His willingness to be humble, vulnerable, and without fear attests to the fact He did not live for Himself. Instead of seeing that image and thinking, "Jesus, get up. You have no business washing their dirty feet." What we should do is look at that example of Him on His hands and knees and say, "Yes. That's it!" Because that spot was not a bad place to be; it should not make us uncomfortable to imagine, let alone do ourselves. If it's not about us, it won't be. It will be exactly where we want to be.

Jesus, with incredible intention, got down on His hands and knees. He physically put Himself in a position to serve, a place we instinctively want to remove Him from. But this place merely foreshadows the Cross. (He doesn't deserve that, and yet that's the reason He came in the first place.)

It was never about Him. Every act, every word, every little thing He did was about us. It was *for* us. He knew the place of position He held in the disciples' eyes. But He wanted them to understand He was merely the Messenger; all the glory was to His Father: "I have set you an example that you should do as I have done for you. I tell you the truth, no servant is greater than his master, nor is a messenger greater than the one who sent him" (John 13:15–16).

Jesus challenged their preconceived notions about what a servant should be and what a master should be. He did so because He knew they still didn't understand this concept. And in order for them to continue spreading His Word after His death, they must not only understand it but live it.

We also see Jesus be very intentional in the way He interacts with the Pharisees. He deliberately challenges tradition and preconceived notions again and again.

Jesus and the Pharisees

What I would give to have been a fly on the dirt road every time Jesus spoke with these guys. I would love to have seen Jesus in action with them. Talk about being intentional.

But before we jump in, let's get some things straight. In the eyes of the Pharisees, Jesus was breaking just about every law known to man. To them, Jesus was arrogant and a blasphemer. The fact He criticized them was outrageous. Jesus was a rebel, even a liar. He violated the Sabbath to heal the lame. He interacted with tax collectors and sinners because to Him, there was no hierarchy; everyone was in need of all the same things: mercy, love, and a Savior. But the Pharisees did not see it like that. He was breaking the law. That's all they saw. Jesus did not observe the ceremonial traditions they took very seriously, and this was a big problem for them.

So time and time again, they tried to catch Him contradicting Himself or telling a lie. And you know what I find absolutely fascinating, especially in the account of Luke? It's that time and time again, Jesus is found at a Pharisee's house, reclining at their table or eating dinner with them. It's so interesting. Jesus puts Himself right there in the middle of it all. He knows He's being watched. Luke 14:1 says, "One Sabbath, when Jesus went to eat in the house of a prominent Pharisee, he was being carefully watched." Jesus was intentionally putting Himself in places, telling stories, and posing questions which dumbfounded the Pharisees. It's like Jesus was waiting for an opportunity to teach them. He deliberately put Himself in places and positions where Pharisees would see Him and give Him an opportunity to share a parable, it amazingly (or intentionally) just happened to work out that way.

Example One (Luke 14:1–11)

> One Sabbath, when Jesus went to eat in the house of a prominent Pharisee, he was being carefully watched. There in front of him was a man suffering from dropsy. Jesus asked the Pharisees and experts in the law, "Is it lawful to heal on the Sabbath or not?" But they remained silent. So taking hold of the man, he healed him and sent him on his way.
>
> Then he asked them, "If one of you has a son or an ox that falls into a well on the Sabbath day, will you not immediately pull him out?" And they had nothing to say.
>
> When he noticed how the guests picked the places of honor at the table, he told them this parable: "When someone invites you to a wedding feast, do not take the place of honor, for a person more distinguished than you may have been invited. If so, the host who invited both of you will come and say to you, 'Give this person your seat.' Then, humiliated, you will have to take the least important place. But when you are invited, take the lowest place, so that when your host comes, he will say to you, 'Friend, move up to a better place.' Then you will be honored in the presence of all your fellow guests. For everyone who exalt himself will be humbled, and he who humble himself will be exalted."

Example Two (Luke 7:36–50)

When one of the Pharisees invited Jesus to have dinner with him, so he went to the Pharisee's house and reclined at the table. When a woman who had lived a sinful life in that town learned that Jesus was eating at the Pharisee's house, she brought an alabaster jar of perfume, and as she stood behind him at his feet weeping, she began to wet his feet with her tears. Then she wiped them with her hair, kissed them and poured perfume on them.

When the Pharisee who had invited him saw this, he said to himself, "If this man were a prophet, he would know who is touching him and what kind of woman she is—that she is a sinner."

Jesus answered him, "Simon, I have something to tell you."

"Tell me, teacher," he said.

"Two people owed money to a certain moneylender. One owed him five hundred denarii, and the other fifty. Neither of them had the money to pay him back, so he canceled the debts of both. Now which of them will love him more?"

Simon replied, "I suppose the one who had the bigger debt forgiven."

"You have judged correctly," Jesus said.

Then he turned toward the woman and said to Simon, "Do you see this woman? I came into your house. You did not give me any water for my feet, but she wet my feet with her tears and wiped them with her hair. You did not give me a kiss, but this woman, from the time I entered, has not stopped kissing my feet. You did not put oil on my head, but she has poured perfume on my feet. Therefore, I tell you, her many sins have been forgiven—for she loved much. But he who has been forgiven little loves little."

Then Jesus said to her, "Your sins are forgiven."

The other guests began to say among themselves, "Who is this who even forgives sins?"

Jesus said to the woman, "Your faith has saved you; go in peace."

The Blueprint Tells Us This

Whether Jesus was with those He loved, or those who hated Him, He was intentional. He intentionally put Himself in situations, whether He was kneeling down to wash feet, or at the house of a Pharisee, so He could teach more about why He was here. This is what He did; this is all He did. And if we believe in Jesus, believe in what He did, what He stood for, and what He died for, that belief must spill over into everything we do. It should permeate every aspect of our being. If we believe in unconditional love, we must learn to love unconditionally. If we believe in grace, we must learn to give grace to others. If we believe in Jesus, we must live like He did. We must live with intention in everything we do.

CHAPTER TWENTY-ONE

And Now, the Rest of the Story . . .

Often, we don't get to see the evidence of our obedience until after we obey, and sometimes, we don't get to see it at all. But does this stop us from living an intentional life? What if we never heard a "Thank you," or what if we never saw a smile in response to our actions? Would we still choose to act?

Sometimes, we don't get to see that smile or hear, "Thank you." I would say, generally speaking, we rarely get to see the full impact our actions have on others. Even on a very practical level, when we mail a card or send in a check, we don't get to see how that card made them smile or how that check was used to feed those sweet, hungry children.

Katie didn't go to Uganda so she could eventually impact thousands of people. She had no idea what the outcome was going to be. How could she? All she knew was she needed to live in Uganda, so she did. I'm sure some days she gets to see how her actions impact others, but I'm certain there are days she doesn't. Does that mean she stops acting with intention? No. The reaction she gets is not what drives her; the outcome is not hers to control.

See, our motivation is to obey. If He tells us to act, we do. Whether it's mailing a card, becoming a foster parent, or buying a pair of boots for a stranger, we obey. We aren't in charge of the road. We do not dictate the path it takes. We may never even know the rest of the story. Despite that, we act. We do whatever He tells us to do.

When we began Upward Sports some eighteen years ago, we had no idea how many lives God would touch through the ministry—coaches, referees, children, and parents. God has been so faithful!

And though we may not know the outcome, we may not always get to see the end product, we continue on.

But, in some rare instances, on some rare occasions, we are privy to what God is doing. He allows us to hear the rest of the story.

This happened to me several years ago. I was working at the office one day when someone from our Partner Support department came to tell me I had a phone call. They said the caller insisted on speaking directly with me—no message, no voicemail—he wanted to speak with me personally.

So I hesitantly said, "Sure, let me talk to him." I walked down to the Partner Support area, and everyone was sort of standing around trying not to listen. (But we all knew they were.) The conversation went like this . . .

"Hi Caz. My name is Dave. I'm a Minister of Recreation at a church here in Florida. We recently introduced the Upward Basketball program, and that's what I want to talk to you about."

I thought to myself, *Hmmm . . . This could go really well, or I'm about to get it.* So I said, "That's great! I sure hope things are going well."

Dave said, "Oh yes, they are going great!"

(I let out a sigh of relief.) I said, "Well, what can I do for you?"

Dave said, "When I brought on Upward, I had to recruit coaches, as you well know. I had this one fellow in mind, my brother-in-law. He was great at sports. I knew he would make a super coach. My only concern was he wasn't a Christian."

I interjected, "That sounds like an awesome opportunity! What did you do?"

Dave continued on and told me how the whole story unfolded:

> Well, he actually turned me down a few times. He told me, "Listen, I'd love to help you out, Dave, but I'm not sure coaching Upward Basketball is my thing. You know I'm not a Christian. I certainly don't feel qualified, or even comfortable, discussing Scripture with children."
>
> I told him not to worry about that. All the information would be right there in his coach handbook. He could read directly from that.
>
> So after turning me down a few times, guess who became the head coach of the Huskies that year? That's right—my brother-in-law.
>
> And he was scared to death.

Just as I thought, he did a great job coaching. I knew that part would be easy for him. But what I was concerned with was how he was going to talk with the kids about Jesus. My brother-in-law was really nervous about that part too. We had many conversations about how all that would work.

He didn't want to look like he was reading the verse verbatim from a sheet of paper. So, the very first week, he got out that big, family Bible practically every household has and read the Scripture verse from that over and over until he knew it.

He did that every week for each verse.

When he first started, he just read the one verse. But then, he decided to read more and more. He began to read the Bible first thing every morning because he said it relaxed him and prepared him for his day.

Reading the Bible changed his life.

You see, he told me, "Dave, I had always believed that success and happiness came from making money, and then showing off that money to other people. I often compared myself to others. I guess all the temporary, superficial stuff was what had my attention the most. I was self-absorbed. It was all about me. But as I sat and read the Bible, things started to hit me right away. It said things like, 'Put others first,' and 'Love your neighbor as yourself.' And I began to realize none of those were even close to how

I lived, how I acted, or even how I wanted to be at the time.

"And then something began to change. My heart began to soften; I was able to feel those words and what they meant. If someone would have said them to me before, I probably would have laughed and thought they were ridiculous. You can't put others first. That would put you behind! But something I can't explain happened and those words began to impact how I thought, how I lived."

Dave paused for a moment to keep his composure and then said, "Caz, it was amazing to see how God Himself was having such an impact on my brother-in-law.

"Not too long after, he asked Christ to come into his life. But that was a difficult thing for him to do. He had built up so many walls, and had avoided God for so long, he couldn't just flip a switch. So he told me he prayed. Just like he started reading the Bible, he began to pray. And the more he did it, the more he wanted to do it.

"When I asked my brother-in-law to help me out and become an Upward Basketball coach, it opened a door for God. Through something as unassuming as coaching basketball, my brother-in-law met Jesus. That experience got him to sit down and read the Bible. It got him to take a hard look at his life and think about some difficult things.

"I guess you can say Upward allows people like me to be intentional through something as simple as a ball. See, my brother-in-law didn't have a relationship with Jesus, but he did have a relationship with me, and a lifelong relationship with a ball. And I knew that's where we could start."

I sat there for a minute, speechless. I said, "Dave, that's a powerful story. Thank you so much for sharing it with me. Often, we don't get to hear the whole story; we don't get to hear the end result. I can't wait to tell the rest of my team your story. They will feel so encouraged."

And as we were wrapping up the phone call, Dave said, "I've got one other little thing to tell you."

I said, "Shoot." I was on cloud nine at this point.

Dave said, "After all of this took place, my brother-in-law started asking me questions about Upward Sports. He wanted to know more about the organization, what all they did, and how it began.

"So I told him a about the ministry, and about what you guys do for churches. I had recently gone to an Upward Leadership Training Conference and heard you speak. I told my brother-in-law about you and what I learned about Upward Sports.

"Well, my brother-in-law's mouth dropped wide open. He reached out, grabbed my arm, and said, 'Dave, you have got to be kidding me! Caz McCaslin?'

"As it turns out, you know my brother-in-law. You knew him long before I did. Caz, my brother-in-law is Rayford Nugent."

Rayford Nugent, could it be?

It was. And I was overwhelmed.

God's faithfulness amazed me yet again. And the fact He allowed this information to make its way back to me was more than I could have asked for.

As I sat there, amazed by this, I smiled and imagined Rayford as he walked into his first Upward Basketball practice. I played out the whole scene in my head: Rayford walks in, looks at those kids, nods his head, and says, "Sup." What a picture!

This story of my friend articulates what happens when real relationships work. It conveys what happens when we act.

What I had with Rayford wasn't enough, not the way I did it. Texting, Tweeting, Facebooking, and e-mailing aren't enough either. Having awareness, passion, vision, or a readiness to serve isn't going to be *all* it takes to make a difference.

In order for real relationships to work we have to be intentional. And that's what I missed with Rayford in college. I didn't live like it wasn't about me anymore. But thankfully someone did.

Dave went to Rayford, who he knew was a nonbeliever, and asked him to be part of a ministry. Rayford thought it was just basketball; Dave knew it was something bigger.

Dave was intentional. He was aware; he had passion; he had a vision to see his brother-in-law come to know Jesus Christ, so he got ready and then, he chose to act.

He did it, and you can, too. All those things that have occurred to you over the course of this book have not done so by accident. You have thought about them for a reason. They may have even produced a reaction in you. If so, that's great! We *need* to react to the things we see and the stories we hear. But, it can't stop there.

The decision is ours: Are we content to sit back and *react*, or is it time to step up and *act*?

Book of *Acts*

Do we act, do we react, or do we do both?

We do both.

An *act* is mechanical and robotic if it lacks awareness, passion, and vision.

Awareness, passion, and vision change nothing if we're not first ready to follow up with action.

On the next page is your very own *Book of Acts*. Really, it's not a book at all, just a paragraph, but it can be as long as you make it. Think of it as a starting point—a way for *you* to hold *you* accountable. No more excuses. It's time to act.

The Book of Acts,

Written by _____
(Your name goes here.)

1. I felt prompted to _____ so
I _____.

2. I noticed an opportunity to _____ so
I _____.

3. I heard a need for _____ so
I _____.

4. I knew someone needed _____ so
I _____.

5. I saw the chance to _____ so
I _____.

Works Cited

Allen, A. C. (1967). *The Skin: A Clinicopathological Treatise* (3rd ed.). New York: Grune and Stratton.

American Heritage New Dictionary of Cultural Literacy (3rd ed.). (2005). Houghton Mifflin Company.

Anders, G. (2012). Oxford Scholar: Your 1,000 Friends on Facebook Are a Mirage. Retrieved from: http://www.forbes.com/sites/georgeanders/2012/07/18/oxford-scholar-facebook-wont-widen-your-social-circle

Associated Press. (2012). Number of Active Users at Facebook over the Years. Retrieved from: http://finance.yahoo.com/news/number-active-users-facebook-over-years-214600186—finance.html

Bennett, Arnold. (1954). *The Journals of Arnold Bennett*, entry for March 18, 1897. London: Penguin Books.

Bible Hub. (2013, June). Retrieved from: http://biblehub.com/parallel/john/3-30.htm

Blackaby, Henry (2008). *Experiencing God: Knowing and Doing the Will of God*. Nashville: B&H Publishing Group.

Davis, Katie (2011). *Kisses from Katie*. New York: Howard Books.

Dunbar's Number. (2013, August). Retrieved from:
   http://www.oxforddictionaries.com/us/definition/
   american_english/Dunbar's-number
Dunbar's Number. (2013, August). Retrieved from:
   http://en.wikipedia.org/wiki/Dunbar's_number
Ford, Henry (1863–1947). American industrialist and
   pioneer of the assembly-line production method.
Hawthorne, Nathaniel (1850). *The Scarlet Letter.*
   Buccaneer Books, Inc.
Hegel, G. W. F. (2013, July). Hegel's Philosophy of
   History, 26. Retrieved from: http://www.marxists.
   org/reference/archive/hegel/works/hi/history3.htm
Jefferson, Thomas (1762–1826). 3rd United States
   of America President (1801–09). Author of the
   Declaration of Independence.
Keller, Helen (1880–1968). American author, political
   activist, and lecturer.
Lax, Rick (2012). Artice retrieved from: http://
   www.wired.com/underwire/2012/03/
   dunbars-number-facebook
Lee, Harper (1960). *To Kill a Mockingbird*, 33. New
   York: HarperCollins Publishers.
Ohno, Taiichi (2006). "Ask 'why' five times about
   every matter." Retrieved from: http://www.toyota-
   global.com/company/toyota_traditions/quality/mar_
   apr_2006.html
Swindoll, Charles (1999). *Mystery of God's Will.*
   Nashville: Word Publishing.
Udall, Mark (1950–Present). American Senator from
   Colorado.

US Bureau of the Census. (2013, August). Retrieved from: www.census.gov/popclock

Warren, Rick (2002). *The Purpose Driven Life*, 17. Grand Rapids: Zondervan House.

Definitions

Unless otherwise noted, all definitions are from Dictionary.com. Dictionary.com Unabridged. Random House, Inc.